# A Gift for People

Joe Franklin

# A Gift for People

M. Evans and Company, Inc.
NEW YORK

Thanks are due to the following publishers for permission to include previously copyrighted material:

INDIANA UNIVERSITY PRESS for an excerpt from a speech by Mahatma Gandhi from *The Gandhi Reader* edited by Jack Homer.

THE NEW YORK TIMES for an excerpt of a piece by John O'Connor from the May 21, 1976, edition of *The New York Times*.

THE NEW YORKER for excerpts from "Broadway Joe" by William Whitworth. Reprinted by permission; © 1971 *The New Yorker Magazine*, Inc.

ALFRED A. KNOPF, INC. for an excerpt from *Mr. Dooley's America: A Life of Finley Peter Dunne* by Elmer Ellis.

M. Evans and Company titles are distributed in the United States by the J. B. Lippincott Company, East Washington Square, Philadelphia, Pa. 19105; and in Canada by McClelland & Stewart Ltd., 25 Hollinger Road, Toronto M4B 3G2, Ontario.

*Library of Congress Cataloging in Publication Data*
Franklin, Joe.
A gift for people.

1. Franklin, Joe. 2. Broadcasters—United States—Biography. I. Title.
PN1990.72.F7A33 791.45'092'4 [B] 77-26258
ISBN 0-87131-244-1



Design by Al Cetta

Manufactured in the United States of America

9 8 7 6 5 4 3 2 1

To my first boss,
Martin Block, of the "Make Believe Ballroom,"
who paved the way for all the disc jockeys
and talk show hosts who followed.

# Contents

*

# Introduction

*

I am privileged to be a sucker. The man hasn't been born who can't put the touch on me. To mimic one of my heroes: I never met a man I didn't like to do something for. The funny thing is, people have done more for me than I have for them.

They say I've got a knack for dealing with the little guys along with the big shots. A gift for people. Now, you may have a gift for running marathons or speaking the French language or knitting sweaters. All of us have some gift or other. Since I can't identify what my particular way with people may be, I'll go along with what they say. Only, remember, the last thing I'll claim is that I should be a model for anybody. All I intend to do in this book is tell you how I feel about people, about life, about family and friends, and I'll let you read between the lines and see if you find inspiration or just perspiration in what I have to say.

Few people get their education the way I did. Most go to school and maybe college and listen to thirty or forty teachers speak at them for five or ten years. Then they get a diploma and settle down to the business of making a living or raising a family.

In my case, school has never been out. Seven or eight people lecture me every day about their specialties: hypnotism, or glass blowing, playing the violin, or playing baseball. And I'm supposed to absorb enough of what they have to say to ask them sensible questions on my TV show. This goes on seven days a week. Throw in a dash of radio talk shows in the wee small hours of the morning, and you've got a sort of instant college of small doses of universal knowledge. After twenty-five years of this—on TV alone—I figure I've been educated by about 65,000 very smart people.

I'm privileged to be a sucker for listening to what people have to say. And what luck! Who else in history has ever had the benefit of being exposed to all that knowledge? The more I think about it, the more I think I should be a whole lot smarter than I am. Instead, I'm corny, I drive people to distraction by changing the subject at the most outrageous times, and I fail to ask the "penetrating" questions that everybody expects of the incisive talk-show host. But I'm also quite proud of myself for having done something in my field that nobody else has done or is likely to do: I've had a television show, in the world's major market, continuously for a quarter of a century. I think the reason I've survived that long is that I have respect for people. To paraphrase somebody else's line: I've seen people, and they work.

I want to tell you about my world of people. It's a world I didn't have to travel to; it came to me. And I think it's a world you'll enjoy. Tennyson said it, in *Ulysses:*

> I am a part of all that I have met;
> Yet all experience is an arch wherethrough
> Gleams that untraveled world, whose margin fades
> For ever and for ever when I move.

# A Gift for People

# One

*

# Always Say Yes

A word that I would give you if I had only one word to give. A thought, an attitude, a way of life. The sound that birds make when they sing just before dawn. The first expression a baby distinguishes from its mother's lips. *Yes.*

Let me recite its forms for you. Yes, I can. Yes, you can. Yes, he, she, or it can. Yeah, uh huh, yep. *Yes* is singular; *no* is plural. *Yes* is personal, individual, intense. *No* is impersonal, remote, diffuse. And all this isn't just linguistic legerdemain, for if you get in the habit of *saying* yes you start *thinking* yes. *Yes* is easy to say; easiest of all when you mean it; when it's part of you, it almost says its own name.

Now, this is no easy subject. Or rather, it's so simple a thing that it ties us up in knots trying to explain it. So I'll be approaching it from every side and from many angles, and sometimes I may say silly-sounding things to try to get close to the kernel. And sometimes I'll say too much, become too scientific, or give too much background. So if I ramble or reminisce too much, turn the pages a little faster and try to put up with me as I do my best to explain this very important concept.

But, after all, this is my chance to say things to you that I haven't been able to say before. I want to tell you the things I believe in, so along the way I'll have to say something about myself, my family, my friends, my work. Bear with me if I drop a few names. I'm not trying to impress you; it's part of my job. Be patient if I tell stories you've heard before; they may be new to someone else.

**It's my very first conviction that all good things begin with that three-letter word, yes.** An important corollary is that all bad things go away without anyone having to say no. People who go around saying no all the time are only using language to make themselves feel more important. They've already made up their hearts to be negative; they say no just because they want people to hear it and react.

About the nicest thing you can say about someone is that he or she is upbeat. Once Bing Crosby was rattling off the names of many people who were important in his life, and when he came to Connie Boswell he wanted to give her full marks. Without a moment's hesitation he described her simply as being "always up." Eddie Cantor was so up he made upness his trademark, but it wasn't put on. He had what the youth of America now calls a natural high. Creative people tell me that sometimes they're so naturally high, so positive, that they have to read the newspaper or have a drink to calm down. In any case, that may be the only good thing about bad news: It's a tranquilizer to steady us when we get too high.

I actually shudder at the thought of having to say no to someone. William Whitworth wrote a profile on me in *The New Yorker* recently, and sensed the desperation I feel when I'm backed into a corner painted with No, No, No. It sounds cruel and dishonest, but try not to judge me too fast. As Whitworth describes it, this is how I face telling people I'd like to help that I can't—

> Joe seems to have four basic types of response to a call. Type D, for the person Joe doesn't want to talk to and can risk insulting, consists of simply handing the phone to Happy or Pop or any other convenient bystander. "Tell him I have a sore throat and can't talk," Joe will say. . . . Type C goes, "Hello? Uh, I'm just rushing out to tape my show. I'll call you Saturday between two and six. Wait for me!" . . . In this case, Joe feels kindly toward the caller but wants to dodge the request he is making. Joe won't return the call, and he hopes that by Saturday the caller will have abandoned his idea. A variation of Type C is for the caller who vehemently insists that Joe meet him somewhere. Rather than waste time arguing, Joe simply agrees to the appointment and then doesn't show up. "On practically any afternoon, I have people waiting for me in three or four restaurants and offices around town," Joe said recently. "I just never go. And you know what I find out? Life continues."

Don't go away! Now Whitworth gets to the good news. I'll come back and explain this later.

> In a Type B response, Joe tells the caller that he isn't doing any booking, because the show is in reruns for several days or weeks. This white lie is for the press agent or book publisher who has sent Joe some good guests in the past but who, at the moment, is pushing someone of no interest to Joe. Joe hates to give such a person a flat no.

How true! But what Whitworth doesn't mention is that these guys know they're getting a Type B response. They know I want them when the right combination comes along for a particular show. And they know I'll find any one of a dozen excuses for putting them off, without actually saying, "No, your rock and roll singer hasn't got what it takes," until they have that right combination.

Finally, there is that heaven where Y–E–S lives—

> Type A—a longer conversation, filled with teasing and flattery—is for the caller who is important or useful or who is simply a good friend. As Joe often says, these people can have anything they want.

Now, let me explain those missed appointments and excuses relayed via any convenient bystander. Believe me, I say yes to them more often than I should. I'll take a flyer on a young singer who shows some class and, even more often, on a so-called has-been who has lost every bit of class he or she once had. But I'm willing to gamble that magic will happen. When the gamble isn't even close, how do you make people see it? You let *them* figure it out. If you figure it out *for* them, and tell them no, you simply build a higher and higher wall of resentment and frustration. They become paranoid. They begin to collect rejection slips like iron crosses. They shake their fist at Gotham and shout "I'll get you yet!"

Quite often my taste for talent pays off. I don't know of anyone I've discouraged who's made it after all, and I know a lot of very talented people who had to work their way through my school of hard knocks before they were "discovered" by the general public.

Barbra Streisand is the one who comes to mind first. She would come into my office and camp like a girl scout rained out of a jamboree in New Jersey. If you thought she looked kind of funny, you would be distracted by how funny she dressed. But what talent seethed inside her! Her sheer animal magnetism was as striking as the aura that surrounded performers like Eddie Cantor, for whom I once worked. She didn't want to admit she was hungry, but she never resisted the offer of a sandwich sent over from Nathan's. She was on "Joe Franklin's Memory Lane" a dozen times before she got her big opportunity in *Funny Girl* (ahem, also with an assist from me). What a yes-girl she was—and still is. (I'll try to explain later why she and a lot of other stars who got their start with me can easily forget their early supporters. It's not ingratitude. It's OK.)

Now, can you believe Don Rickles as an upbeat guy? He was and he still is. Don was another steady caller who shared our humble offices waiting for his big chance. And also Flip Wilson, Robert Redford, Al Pacino, Bernadette Peters, Woody Allen, Dustin Hoffman, Bill Cosby, and Joan Rivers. Who knows where they really got their start? Their TV debut, I know, was made with me, when everybody else was saying no.

What everybody learns sooner or later in hanging around our shop is that I'm not a wishful thinker or an idle dreamer. And **if I'm a yes-man, it's not because I want to feed people's egos; I only want to encourage them to see their own talent.**

Norman Vincent Peale had a different way of looking at it. He called it the power of positive thinking, meaning you could exceed your personal abilities just by convincing yourself you could. That's an old story, and a good one. Auto-suggestion they called it in the twenties. Emile Coué went around saying, "Day by day, in every way, I am getting better and better." Then the Long Island Rail Road picked up the slogan, with little apparent effect. The way I look at it, we were all born with the idea that the world should say yes to us, and all we have to do is resist people and events that try to tell us the opposite.

I think I learned that, as we do so many essential things, from my father. I remember so clearly the bums and bohemians (the same animal, really, just seen from different perspectives) whom my father brought home for a hot bath and a sandwich. It drove my mother wild. Her home was her castle, and Dad was turning it into a bus station. But he loved those down-and-outers, maybe because he had been there himself once. I don't know. When I knew him, he was a pretty successful guy, a philatelist, who specialized, naturally, in the Benjamin Franklin one-cent stamp. I'd like to tell you more about him later. For now, I'll just say that he made me feel it was the most natural thing in the world for a middle-class home owner to say yes to people who needed a bath.

Then along the way people started saying yes to me. I know my wife and just about everybody else are tired of this story, but it's rooted in my very psyche. As the story goes, one day in the late thirties (I was just a kid, barely walking), I walked up to George M. Cohan in Central Park and asked him for a story for my grammar school paper. Honest. He not only said yes, he was so overcome by the thought of a ten-year-old child recognizing him that he took me up to his place and forced some of his records on me. I said to myself, you mean, all you have to do is ask? I was hooked, not only on the power of thinking yes but on the wonder of old records and old performers and old shows.

Am I getting this across? Don't promise the world, promise something possible. And above all never say no. Saying no ends everything; not saying yes leaves things open. Always saying yes, in some way or other, keeps the juices flowing.

David Fein said something about me that makes the point even better. As a mover and a shaker in the movie business, he's heard from me now and again about sure-fire scripts that are constantly being fed into my front door. He avers—

> You should always accept Joe Franklin's call. You never know where it might lead. And besides that he's just wonderful to talk to. His approach is so refreshing. He has no discipline. He never says, "No, I don't wanna get involved in that." He approaches TV the way a guy sells suits—"You don't like gray? I'll give you blue."

**The undying hope that the world will continue to say yes to us is what keeps us going.** As soon as the doors start closing and people begin turning their backs, we wonder why we should go on living. And that principle my father didn't teach me; I had to learn it the hard way.

Not long after that *New Yorker* profile appeared, one of my sidekicks, who is mentioned in the story, dropped out of sight. We all assumed that Pop was sick, and for messengers and coffee-runners we had to press into service anyone who had the misfortune to show up with time on his hands. Without thinking too hard about it (remember, I have no discipline), I assumed that in time Pop would reappear, with caved-in hat, cigarette ashes in trouser cuffs, and three days of stubble. My son Brad nagged me to my senses.

"Dad," he argued, "Pop doesn't have anybody but you to check on him. What if he isn't sick? What if he fell down in the bathtub, or got mugged?"

"Somebody would've told us."

"No, Dad. Did he say anything about coming down with a cold, or going on a trip?"

"Check his place."

"We have. He's not there."

And so began the hunt for Pop, nee Frank Ransky. Brad rented a car (who can own one in Manhattan?), and we headed for that part of the West known as New Jersey, where Pop had once worked in a box factory and had relatives.

I should explain that my staff generally consists of old-timers who like to hang around a place like mine anyway, and who are content to run errands and answer phones in return for a modest but unstressful living. It's in my dinosaur tradition. Secretaries and producers and talent scouts are glamorous but make me nervous. Pop was 59 at the time.

By midday we had found a cousin of his whom Pop had visited a few days before. He had spoken dimly of finding a place to rest for a while. Another clue led us to a farmhouse of a friend of Pop's, which seemed to have been deserted by everyone but a sickly chicken. We were at the end of the line, and the shadows were falling across the Hudson.

"He's here," I told Brad. It was his kind of place. Dilapidated. There was a small building in the back of the property whose door was open. Inside, we found Pop stretched out on the floor. Above him, on a shelf out of reach, was a half-eaten ham sandwich being worked on by flies. Pop's eyes bulged in amazement at the sight of two familiar faces in this strange environment. He was obviously dehydrated, too weak even to sit up.

"Pop, what's this all about? What're you doing here?" I said. I wanted to hug him, and I confess it was the closest I've ever come to a show of manly affection.

While Brad rushed away for some broth, I heard for the first time how a man can say no to life and go away to die like a wounded animal. He wasn't bitter or depressed. He had just felt there was nothing further anybody needed him for, since no one had told him he was important to him.

So I told him. And I told myself I would never again take it for granted that people will ask when they want to hear a reassuring word. I wonder how many old people in nursing homes have given up just because no one will say they have some shred of meaning to someone. Anyhow, it'll be a long time before I forget the glow that spread across Pop's face when he knew that he was wanted enough to stir me from my comfortable habitat on Forty-second and Broadway.

I can sense the psychologists squirming in theii chairs over all this gushing about being positive. Accentuate the positive, eliminate the negative, latch on to the affirmative, don't mess with Mr. In-between. Is it all just a Johnny Mercer, Tin Pan Alley routine? No, it isn't. No, I don't think wishing will make it so. But **I do think words have a way of killing aspirations.**

There are lots of ways to say yes, even when the reality is maybe, or not today, or sorry. Yes, we have no bananas. Here are Joe Franklin's ten ways of saying yes when it's tough. You've heard about body language? This is heart language.

1. *Smile.* Boyishly, openly, cacklingly. Not à la Jack Palance doing an imitation of Mr. Hyde. Beam. In that beam your petitioner can read your delight or your worldly-wise acceptance of the futility of ridiculous requests. Some people smile as they fire you; don't smile that way.

2. *Tell him (especially her) how good he (especially she) is.* Lay it on. That's right, lay it on! Why do you think you know so much that you know what you're saying can't be true? As I say, wishing won't necessarily make it so, but saying the positive things will keep you from saying all those negative things, which we all know are certain to cause despair.

3. *Change the subject.* Call it a cop-out, if you wish; I prefer to call it a diversionary tactic. When you change the subject, you start a chain reaction in your listener that lets *him* figure out what the realities are.

4. *Talk about yourself.* Nobody wants to hear about you. Therefore, nobody will listen carefully to what you're saying. Consequently, you will have achieved the desired results referred to in Item 3.

5. *Call someone.* Anyone. Don't pretend it's in the interest of your petitioner. Let him or her hang on your words. Let him or her translate your one-sided dialogue into something that makes sense to him or her. Say things like "him or her" over the phone. He or she will get the message.

6. *Ask about friends, family, lovers.* Ask about anyone who means anything to your petitioner. The thought of someone who means something to you immediately brings a glow. A glow is the next best thing to a yes.

7. *Praise the opposition.* Your opposition, your petitioner's opposition. Leave it at that. Don't ever make the mistake of knocking the opposition. That's obvious to everyone as a way of damning them into faint praise of you. Give credit where credit is due. Then what you're doing is faintly praising them, hence soundly damning them, hence boosting both of you. More on this later.

8. *Take action, any kind of action.* Set a time and place. Be specific and firm. Demand attention. Never be vague. (Oh, how many friendships flounder on promises of getting together sometime!) Taking action

makes no promise except the promise that something will happen. Most people are content, even pleased, to know that something will happen. Even if it doesn't.

9. *Have coffee.* Food, drink, and medicine are basic to staying alive, and so distract one from the nonessentials, such as bad news. I have ended many a confrontation before the coffee cups are half empty. In fact, my office is typically festooned with styrofoam containers lubricated with a syrupy brown liquid.

10. *Doze off.* Show disinterest. Absent yourself. Be distracted. The crisis will be accordingly diluted.

If, on the other hand, you're really going to say yes to someone, say it early. Then he or she can relax. Long, long ago I noticed that my TV guests were always edgy and nervous waiting for their chance to interpolate the plug for their book or show or performance. So I make it a rule to give them their plug right at the start. Then they settle in gracefully to the conversation. For good measure, I repeat the plug in the middle of our talk, and work it in again at the close of our dialogue. Like a good story, a plug has a beginning, a middle, and an end on the Joe Franklin Show. I gave that advice to Joan Rivers when she came on my show to study my technique. Unfortunately, her talk series, called "That Show," did not endure beyond its first cycle, but I don't know if she followed my advice on how to say yes.

There's also another time for saying yes—to yourself. In fact, most negative statements grow out of internal doubts. My affirmative wife, Lois, speaks eloquently of the power of saying yes to yourself. There's great joy in knowing you can do something when others are in doubt. And often you just *imagine* they're in doubt.

When Lois was trying out for her first job in the entertainment business, she was the proverbial fledgling auditioner, the prototype of the heroines of *A Chorus Line*. Her turn came up. "Can you do a time step?" the man asked. "Yes, I can," she answered, and promptly rattled off a waltz-clog (not a time step) she had learned in a high school gym class. "You're hired," was the answer. The man was Eddie Elkort, now an MCA executive. Legs never hurt, but neither did Lois's self-confidence. **Never say you can't do it. Never say you're sorry, you don't know that one.**

The feeling of self-confidence, one of life's greatest joys, is something timeless and imperturbable, as in John Keats' "Ode on a Grecian Urn"—

> Heard melodies are sweet, but those unheard
> Are sweeter; therefore, ye soft pipes, play on;
> Not to the sensual ear, but, more endeared,
> Pipe to the spirit ditties of no tone:
> Fair youth, beneath the trees, thou canst not leave
> Thy song, nor ever can those trees be bare;
> Bold lover, never, never canst thou kiss,
> Though winning near the goal—yet, do not grieve;
> She cannot fade, though thou hast not thy bliss,
> For ever wilt thou love, and she be fair!

Your self-image is unimpaired by time and misfortune, and more intense than the glaze on an urn. So always say yes, keeping in mind the wisdom of the creator of *Alice in Wonderland*, Lewis Carroll, more properly the Reverend Charles Dodgson—

Do you ever play at games? Or is your idea of life "Breakfast, lessons, dinner, lessons, tea, lessons, bed, lessons, breakfast, lessons," and so on? It is a very neat plan of life and almost as interesting as being a sewing machine or a coffee grinder.

# Two
*

# Be Like the Sun

Be a clown. Be a thousand clowns. Be mine. Be like the sun, and shine on everyone. But no matter what, don't be *on*. That's what I try to tell people when they ask, "How do you do it?"

People often want to know the magic formula for getting celebrities to talk about things they wouldn't even tell their grandchildren. A colleague of mine at the radio station, Barry Farber, says I Franklinize them. He pictures my guests strapped to hospital beds and force-fed huge doses of dextrose. Less polite critics say I butter them up. I really don't know whether it's sugar or butter, but I do know that when people talk to you, they want the sun shining on themselves, not on you.

You can tell instantly when a performer (or a house

guest or a PTA speaker) is *on*. He's rehearsed his act. He's at the center of the world, which means everybody else is in the supporting cast. And nobody enjoys being a bit player for very long.

There are three big B's in my professional life: Bing, the Babe, and Shirley Temple Black. I never met Babe Ruth except through the eyes of his widow, Clare, but I've had Bing Crosby and Shirley Temple Black on my TV show many times, and I've eavesdropped on their movies at every opportunity. Those three people spread sunshine wherever they go (and for Babe and Bing, I do mean the present tense). From the day my eyes and ears started working, I've wanted to be like them. And to the small extent I've succeeded, I am also sunshine to others.

Rick Devlin, Vice President and General Manager of WOR Radio, will testify to the enormous influence of a warm, outgoing personality on the station. After a typical radio show of mine he gets calls from women who think they're in love with me; I am youthful in their eyes.

A dozen years ago I was invited to the Long Island home of a famous inventor, who gave me a tour of his workshop while his wife prepared dinner. I noticed a portrait of a young pianist prominently displayed over his desk. It might have been painted from a photograph of the inventor in his school days, years earlier. Over dinner I remarked, out of earshot of my host, that I didn't know he had played the piano in his youth. No, he just took it up lately, my hostess said. But the painting in the workshop—I thought that might be of him, I said. She patted my arm knowingly and whispered, I painted that last year. That's how he looks through the eyes of love.

Clare Ruth carried a picture of the Babe around with her, in her heart, that never grew old. Just before she died, she paid me the highest compliment I have ever received. In great pain, she came down to the television studio with her old friend, writer John Vegara, and taped a show that had me mumbling in awe for weeks. The compliment was that she had chosen my little show over all the networks, which were clambering after her for the true story of the Bambino. For me, it was a twelve on a scale of ten. Against the background of all the pesky cynics who would like to picture Babe as a carousing playboy, Mrs. Ruth's straightforward honesty shone out like Joan of Arc. Or like the sun.

Babe came alive in her eyes. She almost talked in the first person in recounting anecdotes from his baseball career. He wouldn't have worked for a man like Charlie Finley, she said. When he was elected Most Valuable Player in 1923, he was approached by John McGraw during the World Series, between the Yankees and the Giants. "No, John, I would never have played for you. You browbeat your players," he told him to his face. But he couldn't bear the thought of offending even a hardened manager, so he added, "I'm just a kid, John, and this game is for kids."

Here was the Babe Ruth of legend, but he was real once again in front of the WOR-TV cameras. The station's Vice President and General Manager, Robert J. Williamson, put it this way: "The fifty minutes of baseball we had on Joe's show that day were more 'live' than any game going on throughout the country." Clare Ruth relived those busy days in the twenties and thirties when "the house that Ruth built" was indeed his home. She spoke of how he was out at the stadium at eleven o'clock for the day's game—night baseball was, of course, a long way off. And when he came out of the dressing room after the game, sweat pouring down his face, any kid could walk up to him. And all it took to make the Babe happy was a smile on a kid's face.

In addition to John Vegara, I also had two other guests on the show that day—not because Clare Ruth could not have filled several hours of conversation all by herself, but to make those contrasts that enliven the personal exchange. That's a part of sunshine, too, though some people say it's sloppy programming. Or an insult to the star. I say it brings out the best in people.

When Mrs. Ruth told about the Babe's love of kids, one of those guests, James Bacon, recalled his first meeting with him, as a kid in a small Pennsylvania town in 1924. (Now Bacon is a historian of a different sort: He's a reigning expert and columnist on the Hollywood stars.) At four in the morning, he said, word flashed through the town that someone down at the all-night diner had seen Herb Pennock and Babe Ruth coming in for breakfast, dressed for a hunting trip. Within minutes the diner was full of small boys, and while Pennock ate two breakfasts, the Babe signed.

John Vegara mentioned his first meeting with Ruth ten years later. The Babe had been hit on the wrist by a fastball and headed for the nearest doctor, who happened to be a Doc Painter in Vegara's neighborhood. When the Sultan of Swat emerged from the doctor's house, wrist heavily taped, the street was crowded with kids bearing bats, gloves, and all sorts of scraps of paper. "Now if you boys will line up," he said, "everybody will get their autograph." And they did. Who could do that today?

David Bailey, who plays Dr. Russell Matthews in the TV daytime series "Another World," was the other unlikely guest in our conversation with Mrs. Ruth. Unlikely, but perfect. His generation has seen another kind of baseball, so that his questions and comments brought a new dimension to our subject. He pointed out that Babe Ruth has fed our national pastime in ways other than through the legend he left, or the records he set. The Babe Ruth Leagues created some of the game's top players, such as Tom Seaver and Jim Palmer. And David's comparison of what has happened in both acting and baseball in his generation gave us another perspective on Mrs. Ruth's vision of the game.

As film columnist Bacon put it, actors and baseball players now carry briefcases to work. They've made it big business now. Clare Ruth recalled, "Babe signed his contracts in fifteen minutes. He had all he wanted out of life. He was never bitter or upset. What more do you want out of a contract?"

Clare would often go with Elinor Gehrig to Yankee Stadium to watch their husbands play. One day the four were walking away from the park when Ruth suddenly turned to Lou and said, "You've got to rest, Iron Man. You don't get paid any more for killing yourself out there." "What do *you* do it for?" Gehrig answered.

As the five of us on the show continued to talk and time ran out, the magic of a golden era was passed along to a new and sometimes indifferent generation. Even the Babe was, in a way, on the show that day, for that was the day Henry Aaron hammered the last of his fifty-four records out of the books. What would we do without baseball statistics?

Remember, said Clare, Babe was a .350 hitter, not just a home-run king. Remember, when he hit 60 in 1927, the next man was Gehrig with 47 and after that Tony Lazzerri with only 18. Remember, the Babe accounted for one-seventh of all the home runs hit in the majors that year, while Roger Maris accounted for one-twenty-fifth in his big year. Remember, Aaron was at bat about 5,000 more times than Ruth. Remember . . .

But there were no regrets in the remembering. "Hank brings excitement to the game. He fills the ball parks. What did Homerun Baker hit—ten or eleven a year? Hank is good for the game. The Babe would have been the first to congratulate him. He would make us all laugh. He was just a great big lovable kid." And Mrs. Ruth hugged us all and went back uptown. It was a day I won't forget.

Only a man with "no talent" could do my job. An intellectual couldn't resist forming some grand conclusion about the future of baseball from talking with Babe Ruth's widow. I don't believe in intruding. But neither do I believe in rose-colored glasses, blinders—or public relations.

When Mrs. Black last came on the Joe Franklin

Show, she was obviously interested in her work at the United Nations and as "our man in Uganda." She also knew I was an old movie fan, or nut, depending on what you think of the old movies. (I once wrote a book called *Classics of the Silent Screen*. I've got several thousand old movies at home or in the office, and my idea of unwinding is "reeling," as Pauline Kael puts it, at any hour of the night on my home projector.) Anyway, Shirley Temple's public relations people thought I should try to restrain myself from talking to Miss Temple instead of to Mrs. Black.

I managed to restrain myself for three minutes. Then I looked into those sweet, bubbling eyes and saw only Shirley. As Mrs. Black's retinue cringed off-camera, I launched into a discussion of the great old movies she had danced her way through. How could I possibly ignore such a huge chunk of a superstar's life? My viewers would've left me en masse, and justifiably so. Now, believe me, people have walked out on me before, and since. Not long before this very show, Rosemary Clooney had been astounded when I casually asked her how her husband José Ferrer was. It had passed through my mind that there were hints in the papers that they had separated, but I asked anyway. "Don't you read the newspaper, Charley?" she said with a glare. I couldn't think of anything better to say than "My name's not Charley." She took it for a wise crack, rose imperiously, and hiked away.

So I held my breath while Mrs. Black smiled a Shirley Temple smile. She told me that Santa Claus requested *her* autograph when she was six years old. And then we talked for the rest of the hour about her old movies. What could be more natural? She could have my forum and a lot better ones anytime she wanted to discuss international relations. Two weeks later, I received a large package by United Parcel. It was an early-day Shirley Temple scrap book, with clippings, old photographs, notes, and all kinds of trivia. A priceless piece of film history. And a note inside said it was for me to keep, as a memento of our conversation. So much for the protective hand-wringing of the public relations people.

Don't people ever write their own speeches anymore? Don't presidents of corporations ever create their own ads? It's sort of like having a bad dream, when I hear about the comedians who are now rehearsing their ad libs, and advertising types who prepare off-the-cuff remarks for their clients. We don't have to lose all hope though. There's still the crooner.

James Reston once wrote about a certain good man that "he brings integrity into every room he enters." He was referring at the time to Gene McCarthy, at the height of his political career. But that description applied just as well to another off-the-cuff straight shooter, Bing Crosby.

In December 1976, Bing came to Broadway for the only thing that got him out of the house on the San Francisco peninsula—to help somebody. This time it was a three-week engagement for charity at the Uris Theatre. He was due to give us a ten-minute plug, smile, and say how great it was to be back on Broadway for the first time in forty-one years. He ended up singing to the cameramen, joshing his wife about their courtship, and talking a small book about his life and times. The more Harry Lillis Crosby tried to submerge himself in others, the more he shone like the noonday sun.

"Everybody who hears me knows he can sing as well as I do," Bing began, "and that's my appeal." In 1932, when his "B-B-B-Boo" was wafting across the land, he said a college somewhere in the South got the crazy idea of staging a "Singalike." All contestants, Crosby included, tried to imitate the crooner. Bing came in third, which, he said, "Ain't that bad."

My favorite record happens to be "White Christmas." That's corny, but there must be a lot of people out there like me, because Bing knew that's the Irving Berlin song that put him in the stratosphere. Between you and me, Bing sang better than most people. I once handed him an album called "Steve Mason sings Bing Crosby," and he casually did a lyric from each song on the cover, pitch perfect, recordable. But he talked just as well as he sang. And seldom a word was wasted. Just witness—

On Hope: "Ample in the waist—the only pot that doesn't have a rainbow."

On scriptwriters for Hope and Bing: "If you hear a line that's yours, holler bingo."

On trouble: "Go fishin'. The seriousness will abate."

On aging: "Can't chase the chicks anymore."

On Bob Burns and his bazooka (or don't you remember where the GI's got the name for the antitank contraption): "He's better than Hope."

On marital problems: "Usually, you kid or you hug."

On golf: "The only way to play well is to forget everything else. Then you'll never be tired at eighteen."

On breaking a romance: "When you find he's a fink you haul your freight."

On the Joe Franklin hour: "You've pumped me up immeasurably."

It doesn't matter that we've heard all the words before. Like little kids, we say, "Do it again, Dad!" The old lines don't die; they just come from somebody else's heart. At least once a month I hear the old Hollywood line, "Things are great but they should pick up," and it still tickles me. And I use the same old saws over and over, too. It isn't the words that make the thought.

**So my message is, be like Bing and don't be *on*. Hug the happy side of the road.**

An engineer from England once told me that the worst thing you can do is try to make railroad tracks perfectly straight. First of all, you'll never succeed. Second, if you do succeed, the train won't know whether to key on the left side of the track or the right side. So what you do is spread the tracks just a little bit and give the train something to hew to. An auto mechanic told me the same thing about engines. When you're not pulling uphill or under compression going downhill, the pistons slap around, not knowing which side of the cylinder to cleave to. You throw a rod when you're free-wheeling. Be up or be down, but don't be Mr. In-between. But why be down?

There's an old Irish tenor who's been part of the Joe Franklin entourage during the last couple of years, waiting for a chance to reach that singer's heaven that only a few, like Bing, ever make. Pat Joyce is a big man around the waist and in the ticker, but like a lot of the older vaudevillians and theatrical press agents who haunt Broadway, he's a bit out of touch with the new landscape of entertainment, the "with-it" show biz types, and bright kids. He put in a few days in the hospital recently and sang the nurses to sleep at night; I'm sure that performance will be duly recorded on his resumé. He's composed a song to celebrate the "Beautiful Town of Campobasso (Nestled in Sunny Italy)," honoring Professor Di Domenico of Long Beach, New Jersey. And his latest press clipping, from the bulletin board of a group in Brooklyn called "Middle Americans," notes that Pat was a friend of Bing Crosby. "It would be safe to say," the review concludes, "that Pat has reached the SUMMIT of International Fame."

We have a bulletin board in our own office just to handle Pat Joyce's memorabilia. Prominently displayed there is the following letter:

> Dear Mr. Joyce:
>
> Mrs. Crosby handed me your package of songs that you composed. They all look very good, too. I'll take them along with me and if an opportunity develops where they can be used, I'll see if I can do so.
>
> I don't get too many chances to use new material.
>
> Most of the things I do, as you know, are standards and the people who write for the television shows generally lean in that direction, but I'll do the best I can.
>
> I do want to wish you lots of success .As ever—
>
> Your friend,
>
> Bing Crosby

Barry Farber has me pegged. I do go heavy on the sugar. I just don't seem to be able to hide my mellowness. He writes, "You just feel all sweetened up all over your insides when Joe begins his injections of compliments. I fall for it every time. People wonder how girls can be so gullible. Fathers and older brothers have always asked, 'How could you fall for a line like that?' Well, it's easy. Every time Joe Franklin sees you and goes into that clubhouse crouch and says, 'Holy mackerel, you were really terrific the other night,' then you're under the spell. You actually stand at parade rest and beam with pride. He unwraps each word as though he's been saving that word for you and he wasn't going to give it to you until the moment you deserved it, and this is the moment. And it feels good, and exclusive. And the explanation is—you have been Franklinized."

But I, in turn, bow to the master. I myself have been Crosbyized. The last time the Bingle was on my show, he parted with this shot: "Can you travel? We'll do a double."

# Three
# *

# Everybody Needs Tender Loving Care

Everybody deserves a break. And everybody gets one. Only nobody recognizes it until the years have placed it in perspective. Funny thing: We never appreciate what's happening all around us while it's happening. We think the atmosphere was charged with super-atoms when Shakespeare or Voltaire or Hugo lived. We kick our talented people in the pants because they're breathing the same air we do.

I'll tell you about my big break, not the one that got me into radio and TV to begin with, but the one that made me take it all seriously.

One day after a radio broadcast, my bosses upstairs called me and said they were considering daytime television. (That was when TV was broadcast from 5:00

P.M. to midnight only.) Would I do a show? What kind of show? Anything I wanted!

I decided to try something different—unrehearsed talk. I got in touch with an author I had long admired. She had written *Back Street, Imitation of Life, Humoresque,* and dozens more. I had a hunch women, especially, would be interested in her, but men, too, because she was—Fannie Hurst. Adaptations of her fiction for the movies were convincing and compelling. She must have something to say, because her books hinted at a lot more than was on the page, or the screen.

Do you know what? She accepted. Apparently, that very afternoon I unsuspectingly originated the television talk show. Before then, there had probably never existed such a format as two people seated on camera, merely chatting. Until then you had to deliver wrestling, or an organ recital. But it wasn't just getting this marvelous writer, with a big name, on the show that got things going. What she did for me was something more than just lend her name. Afterward, she'd meet me in Central Park and help me get ideas for my other guests. Once Dick Powell joined us on that bench. Another time, Jacqueline Susann. We'd be joined on other occasions by Tony Martin, Rudy Vallee, Nelson Eddy, Gloria DeHaven, Eartha Kitt, Hildegarde, and so many more. I think I miss those outdoor sessions of the early fifties more than anything else.

At any rate, Fannie Hurst really liked me, and that was my TV start. Someday I'd love to write a full-length article about that fabulous woman who wrote about everyday people and their everyday lives. She was once the nation's most popular and highly paid novelist. At the very height of the Depression, Irving Thalberg of Metro-Goldwyn-Mayer paid her $100,000 for a six-page screen outline—which was never filmed. Maybe I'll call my story "Calla Lily," since Fannie Hurst never appeared in public without a jeweled calla lily, whatever her costume. She also drew her favorite flower on all personal correspondence.

I had seen Miss Hurst's tear-jerking movie, *Back Street,* over twenty-five times. The stars? Margaret Sullivan and Charles Boyer. I got that strange thing—an *idea.* I decided to start collecting early movies, the way I had amassed old records to build up my show for radio. Not an earthshaking idea, but I figured I'd better do something on television that had worked for me already on radio. Even then, I couldn't be sure it would work, but I trusted that old saying my father had passed on to me—"When in doubt, do it." It was based on something else he quoted from long experience—"I would rather regret what I have done than what I have not done."

Within six months, I had bought up almost every old film that could be bought, mostly comedy shorts. Everybody was in the stock market instead of the film market, but these were my investments. My antiques. I was like the guy who bought up all the old Superman comic books when everybody thought they were suitable only for repulping. I was repulping the pulps. Only, in the case of the old films, they were not of pulp quality. I was making my own breaks.

And just as planned, the market for nostalgia eventually came along, to find me waiting in the wings. It's true you can be ahead of your time. **It's also true that if you persist, time will catch up to you.** But the biggest break of all is that I didn't turn on my god, nostalgia, for not answering my prayers immediately. I sensed nostalgia was background music, not the main theme. I let it work for me without trying to milk it for the last drop of novelty.

Remember when Streisand came up with that slow, mellow rendition of "Happy Days Are Here Again"? We had heard that song all our lives, as a bouncy campaign song of the Depression Democrats. She sensed the complex texture of that simple tune when she heard it on one of my scratchy old records, and she nursed it instead of banjoing it. That's what I mean about letting the values of old artistry work for you.

Bobby Fischer, the chess whiz, talked about this many times on my show. I don't know anything about the royal game, but I believe the experts, such as Al Horowitz, one of the grand old men of American chess, when he says that Fischer became world champion by digging through the work of the old masters. And I do know that on my show, at least, he liked to talk about the grand old days of the gentlemen chess players who wore tuxedoes and top hats and spoke like diplomats instead of hustlers. New York's own Frank Marshall was, by all accounts, the last of that breed. He has left his heritage at the club named after him down in the Village. But I digress. My point is that a good, healthy respect for the past is as important for "getting the breaks" as is being hip to what's going on around town right then.

Bette Midler was another nova that flashed across my sky without benefit of what newspaper reporters refer to as attractiveness. But she exuded that star quality and, with it, the unfailing good humor that's the sign of class. I could say to her that she ought to check the diploma of her hairdresser to make sure she wasn't a phys. ed. major, just as I once asked Barbra what she charged to haunt a house (and she answered, by the way, "On an hourly or daily basis?"). Bette pronounced her name as one syllable, as Bette Davis originally did, and I especially liked that. She would rummage around in my record collection for what is now known as "campy" old songs. When she came to "The Boogie Woogie Bugle Boy of Company B," she had to hear it, just from that wacky title. Her best album to date includes her own brassy rendition of that unprepossessing number. Both Midler and Streisand turned their apparent drawbacks into assets, and their real break was the first time they realized that's what they should do.

As Howard Gossage put it, "When in the garden of life you are handed a lemon, make lemonade." Take pride in what you've got. Don't try to conform to some fashionable standard of what's "selling," for, as Sam Goldwyn put it, "When you know what the public wants, it's already too late."

And, if you happen to be on the hiring end of the relationship, the advice is, **don't treat people like products to be tailored to the public's whim.** Don't ask people to pander to someone else's taste. Just give them tender loving care and they'll take care of themselves.

Robert Mitchum, who has thrown many a punch in movies, once looked daggers at me for a brief spell, but, happily for me, his exasperation soon turned into affection. He was in New York promoting a film called *Ryan's Daughter,* and arrived in my TV studio wearing his ever-present tinted eyeglasses. Right there on camera, I asked Bob Mitchum to please remove the specs. His instant response: "No, Joe, I'd prefer leaving them exactly where they are." I said, "Bob, why won't you do me a favor and take them off?" As he started to fume, I continued, "Only because our viewers want to see you better—your twinkling eyes and renowned grin and reactions as you reminisce with me. After all, we're on television, not radio." After a tense moment or two, Bob removed the cheaters, and my audience got to see a real live Robert Mitchum, not the half-hidden star who had appeared on a few other New York talk shows that week.

Speaking of eyes, I have a theory that eye contact—or lack of it—can make or break a television interview. Peter Fonda, who had done four talk shows in town, remarked as he left our studio that I was the only host who'd looked directly into his eyes—not at his forehead or nose or mouth or his own prepared page of questions.

Maybe I wouldn't go so far as to revive the ancient adage, "Never trust someone who doesn't look you squarely in the eye," but I might coin a new one for aspiring talk show hosts, something like, "Focus on their eyes. Eyes can reveal what their lips might seal."

Though the above technique and every other skill ever invented be put into practice, there is often that guest who is simply dull. I mean very dull. Chances are he's there reluctantly, because his editor, for example, has advised him that "talk shows move books, and your last two didn't sell particularly well."

The average talk-show landlord grows irritated on the air with a guest who replies "Yes" or "No" to a well-researched interrogation. Oh, those monosyllables! When the program is over, he'll lambaste the publicity agent who sent him such a lousy guest. But it's been my experience that anybody in this world can be interesting on television if you ask him about something he's interested in. The most laconic visitor will sing like a lark if the right chord is struck. If an interview turns out flat, or sluggish, or commonplace, I never blame the guest. It behooves the MC to accept the challenge, work harder, so he can play the note the guest responds to.

Then there's the self-conscious personality. He's a marvelous conversationalist in private life, but he freezes up on camera, most likely thinking of his friends at home watching, and wanting to be fascinating for them. How do I break the ice? How do I get them to forget they're on television? I ask their opinion on a topic totally unrelated to them personally, such as their impression of the preceding guest. Once their minds are off themselves, they'll respond normally on almost any subject.

Jack O'Brian, stylish journalist of the contemporary scene and fellow WOR broadcaster, told me that he watches my show early each morning while typing his next day's syndicated column. That sort of demonstrates that I don't jar people's nerves. Jack claims that silence can be noisier than noise when he's working, and the fact that my video chatter has become part of his environment is an interesting commentary. He observed on my TV show that my mellow (tranquilizing?) voice causes his newspaperman's juices to flow, and even if Jack was using a touch of his famous sarcasm at that point, I still accepted all this as a super-compliment. And besides, when I was a kid, I did my homework to the happy tones of Uncle Don's nightly radio presentation. Nothing really changes.

Another fine columnist, Liz Smith, asked me on the air once whether I watch my own show at home. I answered, "Seldom. It's agonizing to watch the videotape, because I always get afterthoughts about all the things I should have said and done." Liz commented that possibly I'm harder on myself than my audience. They seem to be satisfied, so why shouldn't I be?

I agreed, at least partially, but I still feel that the best ad libs usually come to mind too late. At any rate, my show is on the air at hours when I'm normally working or sleeping.

George Raft, an all-time idol of mine, told me that he never watched one single George Raft movie, out of the multitudes he made. Call it shyness, or modesty, or apprehension. Or maybe he simply didn't care. Oddly, Raft, a natural on a format like mine which oozes nostalgia, nearly canceled because another local talk show insisted on exclusivity. Eventually, he passed them up in favor of me. The term *exclusivity*, I feel, is misapplied in matters of air time. I didn't care if George Raft went on a hundred programs to sell his autobiography. Success in the drive for exclusiveness should relate to the host's line of questioning, not to conditions of appearance. I never make similar demands, regardless of what the other shows do.

To me, everyone is a star and I tell 'em that. I pass around compliments as fast as I can invent them. And even the old ones continue to please. "Sam, you're the greatest man who ever lived. I pray for you nightly. Let's stick together; we'll conquer nations. Your troubles are over. You're gonna be rich, very *rich*." As I've said, that kind of talk has become something of a trademark of mine, and so I continue to play the game. But when I think about it late at night, when the phones refuse to ring, the suspicion arises in me that I really mean those things, at least as much as the meaning I give the words by that most sensitive of all our instruments, the vocal chords. I can tell you you're a king, a prince among men, a man the ages have been waiting for, and you'll know what I really mean by the inflections in my voice. I may be telling you to think how phony that sounds as it applies to you.

One necessary ingredient of tender loving care is staying away from predictions about people. That great authority on raising kids, Haim Ginott, advises us to refrain from telling Junior that if he doesn't eat his spinach he's going to be less than Popeye. And don't stereotype the kid; don't tell him he's the lying type, or the messy type, or the hyperactive type. Actors don't want to be typecast and neither does anybody else. I shudder when performers are told they're not going to make it, or, even worse, that maybe they should keep it up—as a hobby. Once, shortly after she had cut her first album, I put Streisand on with a famed Broadway producer who, to my chagrin, prophesied, right on the air, that Barbra would probably never get very far in show business. I felt the pain with her.

I learned about tender loving care of people from the

masters: Martin Block, Kate Smith, Eddie Cantor, Paul Whiteman. That great soothing voice on "Make-Believe Ballroom" came from a great soothing person—Mr. Block. When he saw how eagerly I searched the files for recordings to fit his show, he gradually turned the whole responsibility over to me. He knew I had a taste for the discs that fit his personality. And here I was, only 17 years old, and with nothing more than a head full of old songs to recommend me. I had hung around Eddie Cantor's radio studio at NBC for hours on end, even waiting for the repeat performance three hours later to meet West Coast listening times. And Eddie sensed my enthusiasm, too—enough to give me a chance writing his scripts. As for Kate Smith and Paul Whiteman, to say anything less than a book is too little. They taught me that you can't put your act away at night. Just as Gable was Gable off screen, and Cagney was Cagney, those giants of radio went out to people in their private lives as much as they seemed to do over the air waves.

I don't really know any talented people in show business who have a public face and a private face; they got where they are by giving out what was inside them. Bing Crosby told me that he was scared stiff when he got his first big chance—to audition for an act at the Paramount. "I walked out cold—didn't have a chance to warm up the pipes. But I told myself I would just take my best shot and hope it would work." Sidney Poitier pushed handcarts and washed dishes during the day waiting for an acting job, finally landing a small part in the classical comedy, *Lysistrata,* in 1946. He doesn't mind telling about how his own nervousness brought him critical attention: After uttering about half his one dozen lines, he was overcome by a fit of the shakes. He panicked and dashed offstage. By lucky chance, his role happened to call for an expression of terror, and the critics were impressed by the young actor's realistic portrayal! And there's the story about Lou Costello's famous trademark, "I'm a ba-a-a-ad boy," having originated in a childhood experience. He was caught smoking in the boys' room, as the song goes, and marched up to the blackboard to write "I'm a bad boy" a hundred times. Halfway through, he couldn't resist a lull in the teacher's lecture to intone his famous line, which he remembered years later as characteristic of his inborn sense of the comic.

A colleague of mine in this business, Paul Mason of WFLN in Philadelphia, told me recently what loving care he got in his career, and how it made all the difference when everything looked impersonal and dead-end. His idol had been Fred Allen, and one day he got the courage to write Allen just to tell him how he never missed his shows. Surprise! Allen wrote back personally, even though, as Paul says, he had no claim on his time whatsoever. And that was only the first of a string of notes back and forth.

Another figure at the top of the radio world in those days was "Uncle Jim" Harkins, to whom Paul Mason had also written a fan letter. One day the young Mr. Mason received a long letter back from him, too, in which the old pro advised the young hopeful to wait for his break. Paul was growing up in Atlanta, which inspired Harkins to relate how he had booked Red Skelton once in a dance marathon at an amusement park in Atlanta. If Red could start at the bottom, so could anyone, he said, and the message got through.

I knew "Uncle Jim," by the way, through his daughter, Mary Marlowe, the singer. Paul said, "When you see her again, tell her about me and how when her father and Allen were right at the top they would take the time to write some kid in Atlanta who didn't deserve their time. Best of all, they didn't criticize, when heaven knows the kid was asking for it! Instead they tried to encourage me—for no earthly reason. That's it. As Johnny Cash says, 'It really is for no *earthly* reason.' "

Those stories of how we all got our breaks—stars or not—are often the things we remember the longest. And they're full of laughs. Jack Lemmon tells this one on himself. In true show biz fashion, he had come to New York with a thin bankroll, found a five-dollar-a-week room on West Fifty-sixth Street (I'll take it! I'll take it!), and landed a meager job playing the piano in a Second Avenue beer hall that featured silent movies. As much as he liked watching Chaplin and Keaton every night, he wasn't making rent money and agreed to double as a waiter. His boss decided to have a little fun at the novice's expense, and asked him on his first night if he would advise a guest that napkins should not be tucked under the chin "in a class restaurant like this." Lemmon hemmed and hawed, seeing his tip flying out the window like the proverbial dollar bill with wings on it. Finally he approached the table and inquired deferentially, "Pardon me, sir, but would you like a shave or a haircut?" I think Jack was back playing for silent films the next day, but at any rate he credits this experience with teaching him comedy techniques to use live and on screen.

My other favorite waiter story is also about how people desperately need people, but this time it's about a director at the end of his career. D. W. Griffith was on his way down. Poor financial management had reduced him to living in a second-rate hotel on the outskirts of Los Angeles. But "the Father of the Movies" had never really received his due from such great films as *The Birth of a Nation* and *Intolerance,* and his friends decided he should receive a tribute while he could enjoy it, instead of posthumously. After some searching, they finally found him, laid out their plans, and were heartened to learn that the old man was in fine form and eager to participate. The only hitch was that the banquet called for a tuxedo, which was out of Griffith's budget. Here was his chance to get back in touch with his fraternity, and it looked as if he was going to blow it. Resourceful to the end, however, on the day of the banquet Griffith applied to a restaurant for a job—not to earn the rental for a tux, but to get a waiter's uniform. He was hired, made a Cinderella entrance in his waiter's tuxedo at the banquet, and returned it the next morning with his apologies for having a change of heart. Unfortunately, he was not to get his second break; the tributes in Hollywood are often forgotten before the dishes are cleared.

All the same, for many of us **the breaks keep coming, year after year, as a result of things we scarcely notice at the time they are happening.** Let's face it. Most of us don't have careers that require any drastic change of fortune. Even in show business, many performers do a workmanlike job year in and year out without ever trying for a big breakthrough—or deserving it. And there are also deserving people all over the place who never get a mention in *Celebrity* or *People.* But remember Eubie Blake? He's in his nineties, which is attested to by the fact that he *composed* songs back in 1899. His fingers must be ten inches long. His recordings of Scott Joplin tunes are just now gaining attention. At some unimaginable age above ninety, he's getting breaks!

Pop is looking for another break at his unmentionable age, too. He's got the darnedest thing, and he'll show it to you if you seem to have an honest face and a passing interest after his first capsule description. I never quite understood it, but I'm told it's everything anyone needs in this world, contained in a package that will fit in your pocket. It's a transparent ruler which contains not only measurements in metric and inch-foot systems, but the basics of astrology, the pertinent information of the Bible and the Koran, much of Shakespeare, and assorted snippets of modern philosophy. He has a working model, which he will pass before your eyes for a few seconds so as not to reveal too much of his secret. Pop has not given up. Someday, his depository of all wisdom will be sold all over the world, and he doesn't want more than enough in royalties to take a good long vacation.

You know what? I'm also waiting for another break, and for the wisdom to perceive it when it comes. Meanwhile, take care of yourself, and any of your friends who need tender, loving care. You can't be too careful, or too loving. Remember, people are dying all over the place who never died before.

# Four
*

# Good News Comes in Large Doses

What's the best news you've ever received? She said yes, she said yes, she said yes, she didn't say no. Am I right? Or, *he* said yes, he said yes, he didn't say no. You worry about the little things, you fear calamity, but when good news comes it's a blockbuster: You got the job! You just found out that the man of your dreams is as rich as Croesus, and even loves you! You're going to have a baby! You're *not* going to have a baby!

How did you meet your wife/husband/lover/old man/old lady? Isn't that story worth telling? I use it as a test. Even if the facts are as dry as dust, everyone seems to come up with a little extra twist that tells me it was good news.

Lois and I met through a newspaper ad. No, it's not what you think. There we were, two souls in Manhattan about as likely to run into each other as the IRT and the BMT. I had just begun my radio show, and had the megalomaniacal thought that I needed a secretary. After all, everybody else had one. Meanwhile, across town, Lois was pondering her checkbook. Her roommate had just moved out for the summer, leaving her with all the rent to pay. Her theatrical booking business, never colossal, was headed for oblivion. She decided to apply for a job. But most of her skills were the vague ones of show business, since she'd been a singer and a model, than the more immediately lucrative ones of the secretary. Nothing checked out in the newspaper want ads. So she decided to place a position-wanted ad as a model. The only trouble, she discovered, was that the stuffy *New York Times,* the single girl's friend, required that a woman applying for a job in modeling had to add that protective word *draped,* or else who was to know what the lady might be offering? That irked Lois no end. So she told the *Times* that she was applying for a part-time secretarial job. Fine, how was that ad to be worded? "Attractive model, draped, wants part-time job as receptionist or secretary." The scene switches back now to my office, where that very sentence was leaping at me from the page in my hands. I leave the rest to your imagination. My son Brad is wont to say, "I owe my life to the *New York Times.*"

Bing Crosby volunteered to our WOR-TV audience the story of how he met Kathy completely without prodding. That's right, he met her completely without prodding. She was visiting the studio as a columnist for a West Columbia, Texas, newspaper, when Bing strolled by. "Hi, Tex," he opened. "How about tea?" When I shrugged, as if to say "That's all there was to it?" he answered, as many other Californians do, with a question, "Wouldn't you have stopped?" Well, they had some tea, and then some more. Then I stuck my foot into my mouth, which I can do when I smile broadly. "Kathy, what's the thing that eases the hardships of life best—is it music or a happy married life?" Without blinking she answered affectionately in favor of matrimonial bliss.

"Yeah, if you don't like music," agreed Bing.

"Don't blush, darling."

"Aw, get outa here!"

Now, that team was the biggest dose of good news that ever got together.

Clare Ruth talked only slightly less animatedly about her first encounter with the Babe. She was doing a show in Washington, D.C., and had some interest in baseball through her cousin, Johnny Mize. A matinee was canceled, and the cast had a chance to see the Yankees or go back to their boarding house to swelter in the July heat of the capital. Clare went to the game, and sat close enough to the visiting team's dugout to get an introduction to the Yankee star after the game.

"The way they do it in the movies never seems to live up to the reality," she said to me. "It was a dream come true. It was ten years compressed into one blissful moment."

It took many years to get from the first introduction to the altar, just as it did for Ida and Eddie Cantor. And remember how Ernie Kovacs had that bright young singer on his TV show for so long, until he made Edie Adams say yes? That's OK. Good news builds slowly, gathers momentum, then breaks out like the sun after an April shower.

I'm not pushing for long engagements, just noting that sometimes they work best. The saddest love stories in the world are the unheard melodies, the romances that go on too long and end on sour notes. Let me tell you about Mabel Normand and Mack Sennett.

In June of 1915, a top movie director of the day and his leading lady set a marriage date. They had worked together for years and had reached a peak of artistic accomplishment in a very young medium. Their admiration for each other had grown into a love that only the daily demands of their art could distract them from.

Mabel was open, naïve, a little girl in a long dress. Sennett was a man of the world, suave, skeptical. In her trusting fashion, the bride-to-be asked her fiancé to take a look at an old friend who had roomed with her when both were models in New York. "She's had hard luck, boss. Give her a break for me."

The wedding date approached, and so did other members of the company to whisper to Mabel that some young model was setting her sights on Mack. Others advised her that it was just bachelor's palsy. Let him have his last fling, if that would put him in a better mood. But the rumors grew stronger, like the aromas of bouillabaisse in the refrigerator. So Mabel decided to talk to the girl.

After her talk she was ashamed of herself. Of course, nothing was going on. She headed back home to Los Angeles with a sigh of relief. But now let Gene Fowler tell the story.

As she entered her own apartment, she realized that her handbag was missing. Thinking she had left it at her friend's house, she put in a telephone call. There was no answer. She started to undress, for she was tired; but the missing bag worried her. She decided to drive back to recover it.

There was no response to Mabel's knock. She heard the phonograph playing upstairs. She went around the house and entered by the back door. She walked into the kitchen, then into the living room. No one was there. Mabel went upstairs. She heard Sennett's voice inside the bedroom. She opened the door.

It was said that Miss Normand repaired to a friend's house, that of Fatty Arbuckle, and lay as in a coma for three days. Flowers and messages appeared hourly from the distraught Sennett. Finally it was decided, through the intercession of friends, that Mabel's contract would be played out and that would be it. That *was* it.

Mabel died only fifteen years later, the victim of hard living and maltreatment by her public and her profession. Sennett called me a year before he himself died, much later, and said he would like to add to my growing scrapbook of Hollywood memorabilia. A carton arrived by United Parcel a week later. Inside were all the photographs he and Mabel had exchanged, including the ones she had delivered back to him after the breakup. Love notes scribbled on the back of glossies had been trimmed left and right to fit envelopes. Some were folded and had coffee stains. To me, though, it's a monument to human folly, this great unrequited love. Héloïse and Abélard. Romeo and Juliet. Why do we revel in your distress?

The heartache of the breakup of a love affair comes to everyone, sooner or later. Endless numbers of books are available to advise us how to heal the wounds, to make a new start, to make an old start. They tell us to rush right back in to some sort of human exchange, to show the man up with a better man, or to relish the feelings of rejection in an orgy of masochism. I lean to the view that good news washes out the bad. The rejected lover should proceed to some higher level of accomplishment, or at least frequent the places where such accomplishment might take place.

**You've got to "hang out" to make connections.** Most people who wander into my place are doing just that—hanging out. I'm like Joe the bartender, without the bar. They just sit there, occasionally accepting coffee or bringing in a sandwich, which practice I encourage. And they wait for something to happen. They listen to the phone ring. They hear good news and they see bad news, at least bad relative to them. They imagine what's happening on the other end of the line. They know only one thing for sure: They are a part of something that's happening. Some hang around with nothing to say for weeks. They audit the course, and they leave when they choose to leave, having graduated. Then they are free to come back for postgraduate work.

Because I was once on the hanging-out end of it, I have a feeling for how this works. Within the first couple of years that I was on the fringes of the radio business, I had sought out the people who seemed to know what they were doing. The late Ted Collins was managing Kate Smith, and was on top of the heap. Their company, called Ka-Ted, produced radio's top variety program, "The Kate Smith Hour." Their very casual arrangement, sealed only by a handshake, had made them both multimillionaires.

By hanging out, I finally became such a familiar face to Ted that he allowed me to follow him to his private barber and continue talking along the way. A heavy lather was being sculpted from his face when the phone rang. He laid it on thick: "Let the guy wait—tell him I'm with Joe Franklin!"

Now, be honest. Wouldn't that have thrown you? I'll tell you, he was a friend, he was good news. I smiled all the way home. I smiled the next morning telling my buddies about it. I'm still smiling telling you.

Tomorrow take note of people walking down the street toward you, especially after lunch. There's a girl giggling and bubbling, all alone. Her eyes are glazed over, and not from several wines. She doesn't see anything except the moment sealed in her private screening room. Perhaps it was that last reach of a hand across the table, or that shared laughter over her funny story. But she will relive it all afternoon, and will want to share it with someone else she is close to before the glow dies. And when she does, her good friends will let her have her moment to the fullest, in the public screening room.

If anything fails to stir me, it's a parody of all the emotions we're talking about. It's so easy to treat it all lightly. Thomas Hood rhymed his way to brief popularity with this kind of verse in the last century in England:

Young Ben he was a nice young man,
A carpenter by trade;
And he fell in love with Sally Brown,
Who was a lady's maid.

But as they fetched a walk one day,
They met a press-gang crew;
And Sally she did faint away
Whilst Ben he was brought to.

. . . . . . . . . . . . . . . . . . . . . . . . . . . . . . . . . . . . . . . . . . .

Now Ben he sailed to many a place
That's underneath the world
But in two years the ship came home
And all her sails were furled.

But when he called on Sally Brown,
To see how she got on,
He found she'd got another Ben
Whose Christian name was John.

"O Sally Brown, O Sally Brown,
How could you serve me so?
I've met with many a breeze before
But never such a blow."

. . . . . . . . . . . . . . . . . . . . . . . . . . . . . . . . . . . . . . . . . . .

And then he tried to sing "All's Well,"
But could not though he tried;
His head was turned, and so he chewed
His pigtail till he died.

His death, which happened in his berth,
At forty-odd befell;
They went and told the sexton, and
The sexton tolled the bell.

I noticed that this sort of doggerel has since been much improved on in such publications as *The Harvard Lampoon* and *Mad* magazine. Not to mention in any number of limericks that a good Oxford man will recite to you upon request. There is more talent around now than at any time in history. And that's the good news.

I also get good news in a big dose when people pop into town with a day or an afternoon to spare and volunteer to go on the show unscheduled.

Buddy Hackett will always call. Woody Allen loves to come in just to rummage through my library of junk. Paul Newman digs silent movies so much he'll agree to an appearance to see a particular film clip. But the unrecognized talent walking around is immense, too. The big names are maybe a plane above the others, but there isn't much distance between planes. The bigger the star, the better he or she understands that.

**The good news is also that talent is better taken care of now than it ever was.** I remember with pain the day I met an old film comedian at the Hotel Maryland near the NBC building in New York. I suppose only someone who had seen silent comedies over and over would have recognized Harry Gribbon. But I knew of the hundreds, maybe thousands, of comedies he had made, as either star or co-star. Like the others, he had depended on pratfalls, racing automobiles, and hairbreadth escapes from careening trains and toppling buildings, to make his audience laugh.

But then—this is only my theory—along came the animated cartoons. Mickey Mouse and his escapades had more appeal to that particular funny bone than flesh-and-blood performers. Disney and his like put the comedians out of business. Not intentionally, but effectively. Gribbon was penniless; worse, he shared that false pride of a true craftsman about taking charity. From him I learned how much cigarette money means to someone who has lost the good news. Bud Abbott, too, for all his success with Lou Costello in radio and films, was also nearly broke when he died.

We're now doing better by our performers. Bing Crosby, for one, moved his peers to set up something better than charity for those who never dreamed of the word *residuals*.

I've personally had the pleasure of seeing my early idols of the screen come on the TV show and prove in person that their movie personalities weren't a sham. In fact, the boyhood image I had built of them were only reinforced and strengthened as I met them in the flesh. There were Gene Autry, Tex Ritter, Tim McCoy, Sunset Carson, William Boyd, Roy Rogers, and Dale Evans—all excellent guests. For every down-and-outer there are a hundred performers who have grown in charm and accomplishment over the years. And that's also good news.

I once fell asleep at the preview of a Jimmy Stewart picture—seated next to Jimmy Stewart. I was embarrassed. Then Jimmy nudged me. "You didn't miss anything, partner," he drawled. "The best is still to come."

Yes, it is.

# Five

*

# Unpaved Earth and Phones That Never Ring

Unpremeditated art needs no introduction. It's naturalness. It's the feeling that the canvas was just waiting for the hand to paint it. A Dong Kingman vision of the San Francisco skyline. Saul Bellow talking. Muhammad Ali sparring. Grace Kelly wearing queenly robes. Some things seem to be natural to some people. And with that bow, let me explain why I'm at odds with the country. Not the nation country, but the out-of-the-city country.

I was born in New York City, up in the Bronx. I grew up on cobblestones, skated on cracking concrete, pitched pennies against brick walls, played hopscotch on blacktop schoolyards, hid behind boulders in Central Park, and watched with envy as doormen polished the brass plates on cornerstones of fancy buildings.

The solid face of nature is part of me. That's what I mean when I say that my preference for the city is unpremeditated. And not just any city. This one.

Early in our marriage, my wife and I decided it would be nice to live in the country, where the sound of insects could be heard above the hum of innumerable electric motors, furnaces, trains, taxis, sewing machines, elevators, tugboats, bowling alleys, popping neon signs, peanut whistles, and the eight million voices that provide the background music of the city. We journeyed across the Hudson to New Jersey to inspect a likely manor. It was spacious and surrounded by lush gardens. We could afford it. (We had to borrow $500 from a finance company to have a proper wedding, but a few weeks later we had $10,000 in the bank. That's the way this business goes.) But somehow I couldn't picture myself in that house. We remained in Manhattan and paid rent while our dream house across the river has passed from owner to owner and now must be worth a townhouse here. As a business decision, therefore, we took the wrong fork in the road; Lois was right once again. Yet I think I would have become another person if I had left the city.

A few years later we made a compromise: We would buy a summer place in Vermont. Lois and Brad have spent about eighteen happy summers there and enjoy it immensely. I have an idea of what it looks like from the pictures they have taken, but I've never been able to visit it in person.

The one time I did venture across the country, to Los Angeles, I was appalled at what passes for civilization elsewhere. Mr. Rudy Vallee very graciously put us up and conducted us on a tour of the film and fantasy world down there, but I felt out of place. Elinor Vallee and Lois could enjoy themselves anywhere, in Manhattan or in Hollywood, but the unlikely combination of snakelike freeways and rampaging palm trees seemed to me to be the closest I'd ever come to a jungle. And other parts of the country, as far as I've seen, also have their peculiar virtues, but also give me allergic reactions.

I don't sneeze at the sight of grass, you understand. The first mowing of the spring in the park always brings back fond memories of trying out for the neighborhood baseball team. True New Yorkers must remember that first sighting of the grass in Yankee Stadium, an oasis to the eyes, on a muggy summer day. Brownstones glimpsed through a tracery of poplars or birch, or whatever they are, are palaces to my mind. And all over town, exotic or not-so-exotic shrubs fight for life through the rubble of excavations, through the mortar of brick patios, alongside fire hydrants, in dank wells of elevator shafts. After all, Manhattan is a rock.

**The call of the open road isn't calling to me.** It's a melody that's sweet to some ears but raucous to mine. With Walt Whitman, I hear America singing, but I'm content to hear her singing over the radio. The New York City that I know is everything in the world rolled up into one. It has had to do a circus act that no other city in the world ever attempted. In 1905 it is reported that a section of Manhattan had more people per acre than Bombay—more than a thousand. It gave birth to the first motorized taxicab in 1898, and it's the only city in the world that has been forced to send such a fleet of public conveyances through its streets.

Ah, the cab! The limousine of the people. A river of

rubber and steel flowing up and down the avenues. I once asked a frenzied cabbie why he was constantly darting ahead along a curb lane, only to become trapped behind one parked truck after another. He answered logically, "In a city like this you've got to fill all the available spaces."

On a rainy day, when taxis disappear—to some giant parking lot in Brooklyn, I suppose—we pedestrians must find our way through the tunnels of hotel lobbies, under the awnings of Fifth Avenue, or across malls leading to subway stations to stay dry. Out of midtown, I don't know what replaces the cab.

It's a city that's always going to hell in someone's account, at least to the bankruptcy court. Where more has been torn down than most other cities ever built. Where there are more Germans, or Irish, or Jews, or Italians than in any but the largest cities of their homelands. It's a city that people and businesses are fleeing in droves, where nobody would live by choice, but a city, nevertheless, that is still the magnet for the best people in the world—in my opinion. It's people that has made New York City great. There will be crowds, and crowded tenements; feared and hated newcomers; threats from all sorts of pollution. But the people will find a way to see that life goes on.

People in the country complain about city life here that it's too frantic, too noisy, its pace is too fast. And it's true; in the middle of the afternoon you can scarcely make your way up Fifth Avenue on one of the widest sidewalks in the nation. But is that what solitude is—lack of activity? **I find my solitude surrounded on all sides by human beings.** They are the food for my meditation, if I can give such an exalted name to the meanderings of my brain. I find my reveries there.

As you walk down the street in the company of old and young, tourists, panhandlers, promoters of causes, speculators, shoppers, and workers of all kinds, catching a smile here and a sharp look there, your whole being becomes charged with thoughts. And then when you are fortunate enough to get a greeting, quite by chance your day is made! **That is why I say, if at all possible, walk around with someone—it doubles your chances of getting a greeting.** It gives you someone to share an idle thought with. It lends a sense of purpose to your travels.

They talk about the repose and the naturalness of the country. But what is more out of step with nature than a shopping mall? We can't afford such a waste of the good earth in the city. We can't even afford it for tennis courts. Give me a neighborhood where you can walk to the grocery store, where public transportation is at hand for ferrying the small fry about, and where delicatessens are open far into the night. That's repose.

Give me genuine things: sidewalks that have real stones, curb stones, and not some concrete confection to mimic them. Give me phones that ring for real purposes, not for back-fence gossip. Give me streets that grew the way they are out of human necessity and the changes of fortune, not according to some real-estate developer's master plan. Give me unpremeditated art.

I'm an "un" person, like the cola that proclaims itself so. I'm a stone that's unturned. Unflappable, unexcitable, but also unpredictable, unavoidable, underdog.

And the finest compliment I ever got was when Bob Glaser, president of RKO General's TV stations, introduced me at a banquet as "Mr. New York himself."

**I don't think a city could thrive the way this one has without people like me, who like it.** The more people there are in a given place, untempted by the siren call of suburbia, unmoved by the melodies of ranch-style homes and freeways leading to swimming pools, the more really human interchanges will take place, the more we will see of substance instead of appearance.

Here's a parallel to show what I mean. Our media are full of information on how to lengthen our lives. We can live longer if we take these vitamins, or do these exercises, or cultivate certain airs. But our lives are just containers for what we put into them. What good does it do to stretch the container out to seventy or eighty years if all it contains is mint juleps and eighteen-hole golf courses? How much better it is to work on the content of our lives, the substance of living.

I love to kid people about suburbia and vacation homes, and I get away with it because they know I'm being impish most of the time. But I'm a creature of my past and of some ancient predisposition that made me a city slicker at heart. If I go overboard in extolling the blessings of this burg, give me one more moment's patience and consider not the noxious air, the graying buildings, the desperate ghettos. Consider instead the aspirations that they contain.

# Six
*

# Nostalgia Is What We Don't Remember

New York is the scrapbook of the world, but not the archives, since it's too young to be a repository. Still, its contents are too precious to be a lending library. It clips things from other continents, since its own continent is nouveau riche. But what a scrapbook it is!

Along Fifty-seventh Street, down in the Village, in West Side storefronts, all over Harlem, the best jazz in the world has been and still is played here. Discreet addresses off Central Park West are the homes of people the rest of the world has already consigned to history. Jose Raul Capablanca, the greatest chess player who ever lived, died here in 1941; his widow can be seen daily taking a walk along Columbus Avenue. We expect the old vaudevillians to be here; but the revolutionaries, the poets, the thespians come here to die, too. New York is art's magnet, fixing in its field like metal filings the world's greatest connoisseurs and the greatest creative minds of this day and yesterday.

And speaking of chess, that international quiz show, who has been able to sap the strength of the Russian bear, to strain the starchness of Middle Europe, except New York?

Our stone and steel facades conceal treasuries of every sort. Mr. Buschke's bookstore in the Village, which is consulted for anything rare and unobtainable in Oxford or Berlin. Tin Pan Alley has never given up its loot. The Bettmann Archive hoards the photography of all photography's history. A window shopper strolling along East Forty-fifth Street is likely to stumble on incunabula—books printed before the magic year that began the sixteenth century—or on West Indian curry, or on backpacking gear for sale.

Forgive me this reverie; it is brought on by the thought of how my own collections have grown over the years, how I've squirreled them away, in my uncataloged way, in one humble building on West Forty-second Street. A rough inventory: 60,000 phonograph records—almost all 78s, and 7,500 old movies, most of feature length. The records, especially, are irreplaceable and therefore particularly noteworthy to historians. Paul Whiteman once devoted a whole chapter of a book of his, *Records for the Millions,* to my record collection.

I remember reading long ago about the ancient library at Alexandria, at the mouth of the Nile, and how Herodotus and Solon and perhaps the Greek tragedians were consulting it several centuries before Christ. But it was only a scrapbook, and doomed to be shredded by the political dynasties of Rome and Carthage and Constantinople. I see New York as equally vulnerable, but with a strength in its social and economic structures that will preserve its treasures above everything else.

What if someone could X-ray this fat cigar of an island and report what is contained—its artifacts, its art, its books, its architecture, its trivia, its people of destiny? What an inventory that would be! It would seem infinite—far too much even to contemplate, and that's what nostalgia is born of—the incomprehensibility of the enormity of the past.

Let me come down out of the clouds. We want to know more than we can know. We're challenged by the tidbits of information we get from our fathers and mothers, from our aging friends and young history buffs. I said this as long ago as 1962, in the (remember it?) *New York Mirror:*

> The public has seen too much of Chaplin, Lon Chaney, and so on. I'll draw my material from the silent era's bread-and-butter favorites, what used to be called "programmers" in the old days. These films feature such bygone names as comedian Charles Ray, John Bunny, cowboy star Jack Hoxie, Art Acord, Mabel Normand . . .

I hope to say many things here about Mabel Normand, a favorite among favorites of mine. But do any of you recognize the others? Who has ever written or even thought about those old performers since their heyday? That's what fascinates me about exploring the past. I want to know who all those people were and what happened to each of them. The level of their talent was obvious on the screen—but did I see their early work only? How were their films made, and why?

My taste in old things has always been the same regarding books as for records or films. I was fascinated by the authors who weren't public favorites. I picked up discards. And among the discards were books that quoted names that made my head swim. Tennyson, Solomon, Montaigne, Maximus of Tyre, Abélard, Tolstoy, Marcus Aurelius. It didn't matter that the names meant nothing to me historically, and had no apparent connection with each other. They were as romantic as Tarzan or Tom Mix. The Earl of Chesterfield's famous advice to his son struck me as crass and short-sighted, and it still does. But I found a soul mate in one Thain Davidson, D.D., who brought out a promising title in 1891, *Brave and True Talks to Young Men*. It was printed by a firm called The Caxton Press, at 171–173 Macdougal Street in New York, and that alone was enough to recommend it. I can't say as much today when I look back on it; for it had things in it like this:

> All of our wisdom derived from the philosophies of the Christian tradition points us to the virtues of solitude, a sober demeanor, deference to our elders, and patient cultivation of the classical arts. Little can be learned from the novelties of the day.

That struck me as being less than brave and perhaps not true. But it was a nostalgic trip for me to seek it out once again, to see how ground I had forgotten now felt to me under foot. What I *can* recall isn't nostalgia—it's just facts.

**What we don't remember is that we came from something awfully good.** Things aren't necessarily better and better year by year, and that's a lesson we have to learn from the past. Plastic isn't better than wood because a manufacturer can sell it to us cheaper. Its very cheapness may be robbing us of more than texture and elegance. No, nostalgia isn't memory, it's history. We have to invest all our energies into a subject of this importance. It's not an eighteen-hole recreation.

Recently I had the privilege of indulging in what was thought to be nostalgia. It was a WOR Radio tribute to Irving Berlin on his eighty-eighth birthday. My turntable was the forum. Look who came to my show via their recordings: Nat King Cole to sing his favorite Berlin tunes. And Bing Crosby. Perry Como. Sophie Tucker. Eddie Cantor. Judy Garland. The big bands. And then came Walter Winchell, to narrate the legend of Jimmy Durante. How could that be? The legend of Durante during a tribute to Irving Berlin? Absolutely. And for a very definite purpose. Durante was ailing badly. Did I take away from a man's birthday tribute by sneaking in a plea for his aging colleague? Here's what Lucas Longo had to say in a review of the show that appeared in the *Bensonhurst News*:

> Joe Franklin, in what was a peak moment of original showmanship, asked the audience to remember the ailing Durante. Joe's remarks touched the past and touched the heart. I am sure that many, regardless of their faith, prayed for The Nose, one of our most affectionate heroes. . . .

Thanks, but the showmanship *wasn't* original. It was part of nostalgia—to rediscover what we once had known well. But what makes nostalgia more than just stamp collecting is that reawakening of old values. And it doesn't matter if the values aren't religious or nationalistic or patriotic. They're still meaningful.

Here's Paul Mason in a letter to me about the tools of the trade:

> Keep spinning 'em, Joe. It's so pleasant listening to those fantastic old platters of the days of the 78s, remembering cueing the old shellacs with the RCA "lateral" arm, with the stylus which was so fragile, or the Western Electric 9-A's . . . playing the old shellacs until they were white with wear, and one could click the filter switch up another step because the station would be too cheap to buy replacements . . . the days of the Western Union, or even the Postal Telegraph, studio clocks, Phil Harris vocals, and the kick of "feeding" the network a couple of PSAs because Cedric Foster was in town for a speech, and one would feed his show "straight to WOR."

What a great feeling! **All your life you're building up a treasury of memories.** Everything you do adds something to that treasury, which you will be able to call on year after year whenever you want. And what you can't call on at will—ah, that's the pleasant role of nostalgia. Virgil said it, in the mouth of his great hero Aeneas, about the disasters and misfortunes that would break ordinary men:

> Perhaps some day it will please us to remember even these things.

John F. Kennedy once remarked on the shortness of our memory of great men. One year after they were dead, he gave them. Sadly, he was right.

In thinking about this book I indulged in nostalgia, and loved it, of course. I dusted off things I had forgotten, guests I had enjoyed for the moment and put out of mind in the excitement of following them up with others. I knew them enough to talk to them, but not to send a message after them. What a mixture of talent, and yet how similar in that they were all striving, feeling human beings! Louis Nizer, Gene Kelly, Petula Clark, Jane Fonda, Jerry Lewis, Marc Connelly, Michael Caine, Sterling Moss. Take any other list of ones I've named elsewhere. But add in the people you and I will never remember unless we search back: the first-novelists, the poets, the waiters with flaming swords, the historians with cosmic theories, the people with a cause or looking for one. No matter: I keep coming back to the theory that **nostalgia appeals to the young as well as the old because it's a search, not a remembrance.**

My father knew Frank Harris and Oscar Wilde. Wow! I wish I could have known more about my father, and how he happened to know those giants in literature, and how he got on with them. But we all start too late to explore our past. The phenomenal success of Alex Haley and *Roots* cannot be attributed simply to his cause. Give any man a subject of such drama and he will match Haley for pathos and cultural intrigue. The story is what counts.

One of the biggest stories of this century is the way

the United States survived the Great Depression. I grew up in it, but only as a young lad. Others, I know, were of working age during that heartbreaking period of history. Others had university degrees and were selling apples. And the ones who were old enough at the time to remember the period all report one thing: There was a feeling of community then that has been lost over the years. Radio didn't spoil that feeling, it only reinforced it. What will be said of television?

People who lived through the Great Depression enjoy the search to recapture that We're All Pulling Together spirit. Television hasn't been the voice of the people as radio was then. TV seems to be above the battle. With all its power to dramatize with sight as well as with sound, TV programming is generally out of touch with society. And that's a stronger accusation than calling it violent, or sensational. The big thing that television has accomplished is to *obliterate* the past —not intentionally, but just by the way it's been set up. Regional differences in speech and life style have been mixed in the great blender of the tube and come out homogenized. In ways too numerous to mention, that's good. But it also means that one day there'll no longer be a Brooklyn accent or a cowboy gait.

**That's what scrapbooks are for—to preserve the past since it can never be repeated.** I preserve it for myself, for my own sanity and well-being, by doing crazy things like watching old silent movies in the middle of the night. I watch people who really aren't very memorable: Rad La Rocque, Marie Prevost, Billy Bevan, Leatrice Joy, William Haines, Wallace Reid. And my favorite old song is one that hasn't been hummed for at least fifty years: "I'm Waiting for Ships That Never Come In," composed by the team of Jack Yellen and Milton Ager in 1919. So I make my ears and eyes scrapbooks, just waiting for the day when I can open up for someone else who is intrigued by this sort of thing, too.

People ask me what TV would look like if I was made some kind of a czar and could program the networks for a year. Would I make it a giant, living and breathing scrapbook? My answer is always, "Thanks for thinking of me, but I'm the last guy on earth to try to tell people what they want." All I know is that I hit a certain stride on my own show, and it seems to offer something for a reasonable part of the population. But let me sneak this thought in: I would like to see more of the human touch brought back into TV. Don't ask me how. All I know is that it seems to race off in all directions, more conscious of making the time pass than of what is making it pass.

One of the finest trends in American theater is the dramatization of lives of famous Americans. Harry Truman and Will Rogers have been recreated in a way that defies our powers of memory. They came alive on stage. Tom Paine and Thomas Jefferson are, of course, beyond anyone's memory, and so we have to rely on the historian's eagle eye for their portrayals. In the case of Emily Dickinson, we of course have her joyous poetry to tell us how she felt and lived. But all the same, Julie Harris brought her to life in *The Belle of Amherst* with a greater completeness and vividness than even her poetry, let alone anyone's written description, could ever do.

Have we created a new art form in the one-man (one-person, you're right) show? What a talent these actors and actresses have for making us hear a dialogue where there's only a monologue. What a talent the playwrights of this new form have for blending the recorded word with imagined conversation! Picture Miss Harris weaving her lovely description of a train into a never-ending stream of dialogue. The poets won't let us forget what a thing the old locomotive was. It's something we wouldn't otherwise remember. That's nostalgia.

# Seven

*

# You, Nobody but You

You're much too much, and just too very very, to ever be in Webster's dictionary. You're unique. You count. The whole world is a feast prepared for your coming. You are important to someone, perhaps to many. Even though you're not indispensable, you will be missed. I can't say this enough. Great writers can't think of enough new ways to say it. But it's surely true. And the important thing about this truth is that as soon as you feel it about yourself you will begin to see it in others.

Popular songs have a way of getting to the heart of the matter of this importance of you. Just think of some of the titles. You and the Night and the Music. You Stepped Out of a Dream. It Had to be You. All the

Things You Are. Exactly Like You. The finest thing you can say to someone you love is that There Will Never Be Another You.

**All civilization as we know it has been won by fighting for the supremacy of the individual.** At least in the West, that is. We don't have to be sanctimonious about it, but we do pride ourselves on knowing the worth of every life, even if we don't always live up to that ideal. But it's there as a corrective against the tyranny of governments. We even see it as a corrective against the tyranny of such institutions as marriage. We measure the value of the marriage against this standard: Does it serve the individual well? I find this issue coming up again and again in serious discussions on my show. Is marriage more important than individual rights; and by extension, is society at large a more significant consideration than the happiness of a particular person? I'm not qualified to give an opinion, but I *can* tell you how I feel about each and every person. I respect them all. I see in them a hunger for individual attention. Though they know in their heart of hearts they really do count, they badly need someone to confirm it.

Let me tell you about the Scrapbook Lady. Some years ago she began calling me at the office to make comments about the show. She seemed to know what she was talking about; she had facts and figures about all the old-time radio entertainers and personalities. She was especially fond of Rudy Vallee, and I felt over the next few months that she was beginning to see me as a living embodiment of the great entertainer. It was an eerie feeling. One morning the elevator operator told me that a "lady in black," quite old, had come in late the night before and asked to be shown to my office. Outside my door I found a large scrapbook. It was a collection of just about everything in print on Rudy Vallee.

She called that day to make sure I had received it. And after that her calls became more and more frequent. "I didn't like your suit today," she would sigh, and then she would begin reminiscing. Then more scrapbooks would appear outside my door. I would take good care of them, I assured her, and she would sigh with relief. And when she became excited about a particular hero of hers, I could picture her gripping the phone, breathing heavily, her eyes flashing. I think I understand her. She needs me as someone to give presents to. She needs me as a listener. I respect her for spacing her calls days or weeks apart, but when she does call I listen until she is ready to end the conversation, and gradually she talks herself out. Perhaps I will never meet her, but she stands out in my mind as an individual of great sensitivity, and I am grateful that our lives have touched.

Then there's Herculo, billed in 1951 as the world's strongest man at 23. He's actually Jack Walsh, from Trenton, New Jersey. Among other feats, he lifted a 4,000-pound elephant with his back and a 1,000-pound baby elephant with two fingers, and had a 205-pound man jump three stories onto his stomach. He stops in to see us from time to time. There's also the manicurist who keeps my nails in shape and, more interesting, tells me about the royalty she takes care of at The Pierre. There's the shoeshine man, too, who sometimes falls asleep on the job in the next room because it's such a haven from the streets; once I almost went home in my socks. There's also Gary (Freedom) Stewart, Joe Davis the Melody Man, and Kamarr the Magician, who usually brings in on his arm an aspiring actress as her first introduction to show biz. As Bill Whitworth writes:

> The office is a magnet for people who used to be in show business, for people who have tried for years to get into show business and never quite made it, for people who are just beginning to try to get into show business, and for a vague type of would-be promoter who wants to get something going but has never been able to make anyone understand just what. The latter sort of visitor—usually a gabby older fellow in a hat and a roomy overcoat, carrying an armful of manila envelopes—is likely to have three different business cards, four phone numbers, a mailing address on Fifth Avenue, and two jobs. He's incorporated, he'll publish your song, he'll repair your radio, he foresees world war, he's staging an extravaganza of some sort somewhere sometime soon.

All right, that's the zany side. "Characters," you'd call them, rather than individuals, though they're certainly that. Then the more successful characters become "figures" as their star goes up, but they're still the same person underneath. Clark Gable was Gable on or off camera; to prepare for a drunken scene he'd get drunk. Buddy Hackett is Buddy Hackett when he walks into my office or onto center stage. (He's one of my favorites because he comes back; he doesn't mind remembering where he came from.) The sad thing I see coming in is the star who leads a double life, for whom performance is only a job. Sad, I guess, because to me radio always meant mysterious, exotic, full-blown individuals.

A character who's hard to explain to this generation was the above-mentioned Voice of Experience. In the early thirties he appeared on the radio scene like a comet from the East. His identity was a closely guarded secret. In a sonorous, dignified voice he delivered sermonettes on a variety of personal subjects, such as marital fidelity, to a depression-chastened nation. A sample:

> If only we could hold a mirror up to the really angry person and let him see what he looked like when all his animal, infantile, soul-searing passions were aroused, how much less damage there would be from temper tantrums.

On another topic:

> What are your children doing at this very moment? Are they engaged in a worthwhile pursuit? Are you giving them an example to follow? Do you know that you are responsible for their moral development, for sixty or more years of life? Parents of America, the future of the world is in your hands!

A steady stream of this sort of prodding issued from The Voice of Experience to a weekly radio audience of millions. A profile of him even appeared in *The New Yorker*. Speculation about his identity appeared periodically in newspapers. Advertisers raised the ante for his services. But in time his popularity waned, and this master showman went on to other pursuits. Later, he was revealed as Marion Sayle Taylor, a Portland, Oregon, businessman who had once debated with William Jennings Bryan. A sort of prelude to the consciousness-raising salesmen of this generation, he had conducted seminars and lectured on personal improvement before taking his talents to the airwaves.

The conformity required within a large corporation is undoubtedly a major threat to the emergence of characters like Mr. Taylor. But it's also a threat to individuals of any kind. Decisions are made, more and more often, by committees. Corporate politics dictates a policy of keeping a low profile. If you're noticed as a little outlandish, you're open to suspicion as not being a team player. And the signs of this attitude are plain in the attempts to standardize tastes through mass marketing. The pressure to conform has been documented for many years. But all is not lost. For instance, I can hold out the example of my way of doing business to suggest that it's still possible to stand out from the crowd and not be shouted down.

One of the reasons you can, as I see it, is that **no matter how different you are, your conformity is more noticeable than your differences.** If you're a man, you still dress pretty much like me. Most likely, you eat at the same times. You probably go to work when others do. The human characteristics—fear and anger, happiness and hope—that run through all of us are constantly pulling us in the direction of conformity. Never worry about being too different. Worry about giving up your individuality.

Once a young man popped into the office all aflutter. He had a rock group that was "different." They would make a breakthrough like the Beatles. They would make the audience rush out to the nearest record store. Then an assistant of mine, John Castron, suggested that if they were that much like the Beatles it probably wouldn't be a good idea to come on our show, because we always wanted someone original.

So be a nonconformist. But my advice is also, be polite about it. There's no greater bore than the person who thinks bad manners are the equivalent of originality. Dame Edith Evans once commented, "When a woman behaves like a man, why doesn't she behave like a nice man?" For the men, wear ties when establishments require them. Uniforms have a purpose. For the women, go to the theater dressed for it. Save your nonconformist tendencies for the occasion when no one will be offended. And do your duties to society. Give blood, observe the law, don't fall down drunk at your mother-in-law's house.

Part of the trick is to **cultivate a sense of change.** Don't become fixed in any pattern, even a nonconformist pattern, or you will become predictable.

Picasso is reported to have said, "God is really only another artist. He invented the giraffe, the elephant, and the cat. He has no real style. He just goes on trying other things."

You can do it, too. You, baby, nobody but you.

# Eight
*

# Fathers Do Know Best

For some reason or other, men take a long time to come around to the recognition of the importance of their fathers in their lives. Could, of course, be that ol' Oedipus Complex. Yet I see the phenomenon more often than not in sons who feel their fathers are an embarrassment to them, not competition. A library could be filled with books lamenting lost opportunities between father and son.

One friend of mine recalls at least once a week how he looked down on his father for fighting the apparently hopeless battle of trade unionism in the textile industry at the beginning of this century. The old man had to be bailed out of jail periodically, and was always in dire financial straits. At the time, the son thought the world of music and the arts of more consequence. Now, some sixty years later, it is obvious to him that he had the script backward. And now he wishes only to pass on to *his* son this one lesson of his life.

I have already said how I relished my own father's incorrigible habit of bringing strangers home for a hot bath, and that was just one of the ways we got along. I count myself lucky for that early father–son rapprochement we enjoyed; (it had to be early if it was ever going to be, since he died when I was in high school). Since my father was a newspaperman, a reporter for the old *New York Mail*, I've always had a fondness for people who deal with the news. And maybe it was because I missed my father's hand so much that I looked for it in the Cantors and Jolsons and Cohans.

I remember reading in the *New York World-Telegram* a piece by Heywood Broun about how he got started in the newspaper business. It's funny but his story made me greatly envy that continuum of father–son–grandson that has marked so many great literary families in England and the United States. That many such men who were living full, satisfying lives were taking unfair advantage of the economic system of their day can hardly be argued away. But since it's not my place here to seek reparation, I'll only tell the story as it happened. The younger Broun said—

> My father was in business and sometimes he worked until six and seven, and occasionally he would get off early in the afternoon. But no matter how early my

> father got to the club he always found Finley Peter Dunne sitting there, having a drink or playing backgammon or having a good time in one way or another. And he always seemed to be in funds. My father got the idea that writing must be the easiest job in the world, and when I was nine he nominated me for the craft.

The Finley Peter Dunne he speaks of was, of course, the creator of the Irish philosopher-at-the-bar, Mr. Dooley, and during all those hours at the club, Dunne was generating or collecting conversation to put into Mr. Dooley's mouth, conversation that came out in a brogue that was the bane of all the typesetters in Manhattan. Dunne also presided over a ritual luncheon at the Holland House in the early 1900s, much as in the thirties Broun and Robert Benchley and Franklin P. Adams and the others held forth at the Algonquin Hotel on West Forty-fourth Street. I mention all this only to allude to the ties that most of us have, through one acquaintance or another, with the literary traditions of our century.

One of those connections of mine is someone who frequents our office, Broadway columnist Irving Cahn. Cahn moved in the circle of the Algonquin Round Table as the theater critic for *Metropolitan Host* magazine, and so provides us with a sense of the not-so-distant past that is more precious than all the antiques on Fifty-seventh Street.

And look how the ties extend all the way back into the youth of our country, as the patriarchs of an early period brush with their literary sons. There is something of a father–son chain in much of American writing. In his memoirs, the same Dunne who inspired Broun recalled his own rites of passage with Mark Twain, at the twilight of his long career—

> In New York after the death of that lovely creature Jean, Mark Twain tried to brighten his life a little by going to theaters, having friends come to his house and making new friends with the younger generation. I was lucky enough to be among this group. He always treated Collier and me as if we were still in our adolescence although when I first met him in 1899, I had been a hard-boiled newspaperman for fifteen years, had written four or five books and edited or published about that many newspapers and magazines. He would say, "I like you young fellows. I like to have you around me. But you mustn't expect me to listen to your opinions. They are too immature. Wait till you and Collier have made a reputation. Then you can talk to me and I will stay awake."

But the old lion ineluctably yielded his throne bit by bit. Dunne recounts with pride a memorable episode that marked the passing of the crown to his head:

> In his last years, he, who had once been rather shy, took hungrily to the publicity that was poured on him. He liked attention; he even demanded it. In the streets of New York he was a more marked figure than Theodore Roosevelt or J. P. Morgan. His noble countenance, his splendid head would distinguish him in any crowd, however great, but when he took to wearing white clothes—a sensible thing to do, but a conspicuous one —no one who had ever seen a picture of him in the papers could miss him.
>
> One bright spring afternoon I met him at the

crowded corner of Fifth Avenue and 42nd Street. As usual we stopped to exchange our customary banter about the ignorance of youth and the impotence of age. Thousands and thousands of men, women and children passed us and every mother's son and daughter turned his head to look at the picturesque figure. Some of them stopped and listened. At one time there must have been fifteen or twenty typical New York rufuses gawking at him. Mark loved it. His face was aflame. His eyes shone. He talked better and louder than I had ever heard him. Finally I said, "Let's get out of here and go over to the Century and have a drink."

"I'm not a member of the Century. What's the matter with staying here?"

"But aren't you embarrassed standing here in these crowds, talking to a celebrity?" I said.

He answered like a man coming out of a trance. His eyes were wide open and staring. He stammered, "Wh-wh- why, do *you* think these people are looking at *you?* Why, you conceited fellow, they're looking at *me!*" Then the fact dawned on him that youth had at last rebelled. His face broke into a great grin. "Oh, come on over to the Century and have a drink."

"But you just said you weren't a member."

"I'm not. That makes my hospitality all the more remarkable. What could be finer than to entertain a friend at a club where you're not a member?'

"But I'm a member."

"I knew that or I wouldn't have invited you to have a drink."

A biographer of Dunne, Elmer Ellis, tells a story that particularly made me want to know more about this man and his era. It seems that Peter was a born vaudevillian at the dinner table as a child. One day he became fascinated by a window display in a store where ecclesiastical goods were sold. The tortures of the damned were depicted by some modern Dante in exquisite and gruesome detail. A report of his window shopping reached the dinner table that evening. It was his cue. He launched into a pantomime of each gaudy excess, sending the family into such gales of laughter that dinner had to be delayed.

My younger sister Madeline, "Meg" to everyone but her stuffy brother, told a story on me in a similar vein in an interview that appeared in the *Somerset Messenger Gazette* some years ago. She recalls—

> We used to shop around in second-hand stores for old records, which sold two for a penny. I guess the collecting instinct is in our family; Dad was a stamp collector. I would polish the records for him and catalog them. I think by the time Joe was 16, he had 1,000 records. Amazingly, he could always find exactly the one he was looking for. Dad used to think Joe spent too much time with the records, and when he would be playing the phonograph instead of doing his homework I would call out to warn him when I heard Dad's footsteps in the hall. Joe loved to clown and I was always skinny because he would have me laughing at dinner and I could never eat what was in front of me.

That's it! The Laugh-Your-Way-Thin Diet. I've seen worse. But just to corroborate that account, let me balance it with what my wife has to say.

Ten years ago or so, she was asked by Leo Mishkin, the TV critic, how I got started collecting records. The story she gave is the one I've already mentioned, of the episode in Central Park with George M. Cohan. He really *did* give me one of his records, "Life's a Funny Proposition After All." And I really did go out and collect every one of his previous records—seven in all. In truth, the explanation for my recognizing Cohan was that my mother had taken me to his Broadway musical the night before. But Lois would put it another way. She says—

> Eecch! You want the real story? Joe was sick one time when he was a kid, and his father bought him a phonograph. Then his mother went out to buy some records, but they cost 35 cents each, and she didn't want to spend that kind of money. So she asked the guy in the record store if he didn't have a lot of old records down in the basement that he didn't want. She'd buy them for a penny apiece. . . . And that's the real story of how Joe started collecting all those scratchy, tinny 78s.

Somebody, somewhere will someday be asking how Brad Franklin got started in whatever will make him . . . happy. (I almost said "famous," but that's not this father's wish.) A performer's life is not his own, even as low-key a performer as I am. The world of work and careers has changed mightily since Heywood Broun's day. Who can tell what a young man of today should do with his life? Does a father know best? Yes, if he knows when to cut loose and let his actions speak louder than his words.

Sloan Wilson, who created *The Man in the Grey Flannel Suit,* recently had some things to say about raising children. He said it was something like teaching a child how to ride a bike. A certain amount of guidance and direction is essential, but at some indefinable point the hovering father has to let go or the very process whereby bicycles are kept in balance will be subverted.

I happen to have made a career out of a hobby. My whole life has become like the pot of rice the bride filled to the brim on her first venture into the kitchen. The hobby has overflowed into everything I do. Maybe when I say I don't wish that on Brad I'm saying I don't wish my relationship with him to be his with *his* children. My work precludes my spending with my family the hours a father normally has with his wife and children. And so I have this confession: I can't "fix" anything for him in broadcasting or publishing or whatever else seems to a father to be a plush career. But secretly I yearn for him to succeed, yearn so hard that I would like to be *his* assistant, to be the fellow who goes out for coffee and buys the newspapers for *him*. And that, I think, is what fathers everywhere in their heart of hearts want.

"You are your father's father," said Hart Crane. (He also said, "Thin squeaks of radio static / The captured fume of space foams in our ears." But I won't hold that against him!) Or, as Wordsworth put it, "The Child is father of the Man." **And Joe Franklin says that fathers are taught by their children—taught the things that they, in their fight for survival, had forgotten.** What is this fascination of grandfathers for grandchildren? It's their return to innocence after the furnace of cynicism they have lived through.

The people I admire most are those who in the face of having lost a child to war, or to drugs, manage to continue on. The newspapers pounce on stories of sons of entertainers or politicians or artists who run afoul of the law. Two of this century's greatest comedians, Sir Harry Lauder and Joe E. Brown, each lost a son in a world war. Few people have ever heard about that. Jackie Robinson was another of many to suffer tragically because of a son's misfortune. I admire these people because their suffering is never understood, and if one needs anything in suffering it is understanding.

In the cycle that begins with that first glimpse in the maternity-ward window and ends with the last glassy stare from their deathbed, fathers go through loop-the-loops of efforts to understand their children. At first they are a mystery to the child, until their role with the mother is sensed. Then they are admired, loved, tolerated, abhorred, reconciled, and revered.

Through this cycle, the fathers are tempted by the Sirens of Being Successful, and Acting Your Age, and Growing Old Gracefully, when in reality all they want to be is boys. But they don't fear death, especially if they have been able to pass on to someone, perhaps their own children, what life has meant to them. Mark Twain said, only half joking, "Whoever has lived long enough to find out what life is knows how deep a debt of gratitude we owe to Adam, the first great benefactor of our race. He brought death into the world."

Perhaps the debt that fathers owe their children is best expressed by the childless. James Whitcomb Riley touched this nerve in a long narrative poem, "Tom Van Arden," in which the friendship and good living of two aging bachelors is compared with the joys of having children—and loses. Part of it goes this way:

Tom Van Arden, my old friend,
  Are we "lucky dogs," indeed?
Are we all that we pretend
  In the jolly life we lead?—
    Bachelors, we must confess,
    Boast of "single blessedness"
    To the world, but not along—
    Man's best sorrow is his own!

. . . . . . . . . . . . . . . . . . . . . . . . . . . . . . . . . . . . . . . . . . . . . .

    I propose a health to those
    Who have *homes,* and home's repose,
    Wife and child-love without end!
    . . . Tom Van Arden, my old friend.

When I hug children at ribbon cuttings or open houses, I don't peck them on the cheek like a politician. I hug them like someone I know I will lose someday. That's what fathers—and mothers—know best.

# Nine

*

# Open-Door Policy

Openness is the most telling description of the American scene that a single word can convey. It encompasses free enterprise, social mobility, civil rights, open minds, open roads, and open doors. I don't claim to be leading a movement, but I do practice what I preach, and preach a kind of democracy of the door handle. Anyone can use mine, anytime I'm in my office. Let me quote the very bright reporter, Carol Pearce, since she can say it better than I can—

> Joe Franklin stands in the pale green hallway that leads to his 42nd Street office, looking even paler. He is wearing a green plaid, tailor made, dapper looking suit. He talks intently with an older man, but he spots me as soon as I come around the corner greeting me as though he had been waiting for my visit all day.

(Note how your greeting should be enthusiastic even if you're not quite up to it. The *impression* of your greeting will help improve the *reality* of your greeting. A little later:)

> One or another of his helpers constantly comes to the door to call him to the phone. Joe moves in and out of the anteroom, avoiding as he goes the frayed rope that hangs from a bare light bulb. All the while he smiles a secret sort of smile and occasionally winks at me.

(You already have a picture of a rather modest office. The informality of the place puts visitors at ease and gives them something to smile about. Now, winking sounds rather obvious, but you have to find some way to keep your visitors on stage. Be obvious!)

> At one of his absences, a helper brings in a cup of coffee and very gently sets it on Joe's chair. (Even when he's gone, he's there.) When Joe returns he hands the coffee to me like a jewel. "Here." "No, Joe, it's yours." "What do you mean," he says, "I got it for you." So I drink some and when I set it down Joe absentmindedly drinks out of it too.

(I didn't fool her one bit. She knew it was my coffee, but I knew that she knew, and she knew that I knew that she knew. When the logicians get through with that they'll discover that it all adds up to nothing more than a nice gesture. Fair enough? Let's go on:)

> A man comes to show Joe a book he's just written. Joe thumbs the pages and says instantly, "Your troubles are over." The man smiles broadly, and Joe takes him into the hall, talking quietly, his hand on the man's shoulder. . . . A man in a beat-up trench coat and hat

> shuffles in with two shopping bags, various sacks, bundles and his pockets bulging as well. Joe's friends moan and groan when they see him. He immediatcly pulls out boxes of perfumes and tries to sell them to Joe, who calls him "Shlep" and walks around generally ignoring him. . . . Finally he begins nagging Joe to give him some string to tie his packages. . . . People are still walking in and out of Joe's rooms continually—all shapes, sizes, and assortments—starlets to magicians. . . . Joe greets them all warmly—running out into the hall—dashing into his office to answer phone calls—whipping back to talk and deal with the radio men, making an appointment for them to be on his TV show. . . . He's beginning to look a little tired—his face more pale—he rubs his eyes occasionally while he talks. His answers grow shorter. "No, I can't. We're good friends, but I can't put you on TV."

(Look what you have to give up when your door is always open: the privilege of talking only to those people for whom you have a good word.)

What if several hundred people who read this book suddenly decide to test my policy by arriving at my office at 2:00 P.M. next October 23. After all, I am listed in the phone book. Well, sometimes it does become rather crowded, but it's a self-regulating proposition. Unable to get any attention, the just-curious leave. Confident that they have something to tell me, the serious hang around. If you're Hedy Lamarr, you don't have to come to the office to get my attention. If you're just peddling something, you know that I know that you know what you're up to. And I can insult you to your face—gently.

Among all the famous stories about Will Rogers, one of them very neatly illustrates this last point. Rogers was the featured speaker and guest of honor at a convention of bankers. They had been advised that the humorist had a rather tart view of money men, but they were prepared to take his cracks in good humor as long as they were suitably entertained. He started out with a typical salvo: "You're as fine a group of gentlemen as ever foreclosed on a widow. I'm honored to be with you Shylocks." Nervous laughter trickled through the hall. The insults continued, lightly tempered by words like *gentlemen,* and *honored.* At no point did the quizzical smile become a snarl. At the end he received a warm round of applause—and an invitation to come back again!

A person is like a radio; what comes in the receiver goes out the speaker. So the more open your mind is, the more of value you have to say. I don't know how people can be physically remote, shut off from people they don't want to see and from events they don't want to know about, and pretend to be open to another point of view.

And meeting people openly means meeting them on *their* terms, not yours. **Professionally, I find that the open-door policy of my office helps immensely in keeping an open mind in making that critical adjustment to the guest's own terms.**

Once, for example, I sensed that Bing Crosby wanted to have Kathy appear with him on the shows he did to publicize his Broadway comeback in 1976. One New York talk-show hostess preferred to make Bing fit into the mold of her program, which meant he would appear without his wife. Trouper that he was,

Crosby didn't pass up the publicity, but he couldn't help showing his annoyance. He was on and off quickly and left the studio with Mrs. Crosby as soon as the show was over. In the more relaxed atmosphere of our show, Bing and Kathy sparkled, remaining sometime afterward to sign autographs and trade gags with the guests who weren't able to get on. I think some TV hosts have an unconscious desire to exercise their power over the rich and famous people they interview.

Sometimes, of course, I slip. Once I misread Ernest Borgnine, and made a tired joke about his unusual last name. He promptly got up and left the studio. Comics are my favorite guests, and perhaps I have an unconscious desire to make over all my guests into comedians. I recall that I took Sylvester Stallone a little lightly; I had him and another of the "Lords of Flatbush" toss pies at each other on camera. Now that he's in top shape I'll have to watch that. But I've been quite successful in getting people to laugh when they thought they were coming on to do a serious number: Lauren Bacall, when she was doing *Applause*; Xavier Cugat when he was changing wives; Robert Redford when he was starring with Elizabeth Ashley in *Barefoot in the Park*.

I picked up the open-door policy from the people who gave me an open door, and also perhaps from my first contact with the world of radio and records. In those early days people like Ted Collins would see you and make an instant decision about letting you on the Kate Smith show. The conglomerates and their guarded opinions were still unheard of. And I've found that talented people are generally open. They've

*Joe Franklin . . .*

*. . . in 1949*

*. . . with Martin Block*

*. . . with Liza Minelli*

*. . . with Robert Mitchum*

*. . . with Debbie Reynolds*

*. . . with Tony Orlando*

*. . . with Charles Tobias, Anita Bryant, and Stella Stevens*

. . . *with Brad Franklin*

. . . *with Shirley Temple Black*

*. . . with Luise Rainer*

*. . . with Barbra Streisand and Jack La Lanne*

*. . . with Bing and Kathy Crosby*

taught me to open up to the lesser-known performers as they've opened up to me.

One story of their openness took place about a dozen years ago when an actress named Lyda Arco Long was trying to make a comeback on the stage at the age of 58. To exhibit her talent she opened her modest apartment to the public for a free performance of Chekhov's *The Cherry Orchard*—with all parts played by herself. I didn't attend, but I understand that enough influential people did, that she succeeded in getting back into the theater.

That event and many others like it confirmed me in my habit of watching out for the old-timers first. There's always a place in my heart for people like ex-Follies girls. They've organized. Doris Vinton is the president of a club of Ziegfeld graduates.

Radio itself was an open-door medium, and those of us who grew up with it were caught up in its spirit. Radio not only opened up a whole new world to Americans, it listened to what Americans of all tastes and classes wanted.

When Amos n' Andy came on the air each evening at seven o'clock, the nation ground to a halt. The telephone switchboards were eerily silent. Movie theaters interrupted their films promptly and wheeled on stage those huge contraptions, radios, to play the evening's adventure for their audiences. At first the show went on in the East at eleven so that it could be heard, live of course, at ten, nine, and eight across the country. Parents in the East found that disastrous; their children wouldn't go to bed. So NBC switched the time to seven. More than a 100,000 letters of protest poured in from across the land. NBC finally solved the problem by staging two separate broadcasts, four hours apart. During emotionally charged episodes, such as Amos's trial for murder, even the White House of Coolidge and Hoover was tuned in. And, of course, something so universally enjoyed had the very positive, "opening" effect of helping to break down class barriers.

Also working to break down class barriers were the movies of the day. In D. W. Griffith's words, films were "the struggling art of the common people," where only the theater and opera and the ballet had existed before. *The Birth of a Nation* was shown at the White House for Woodrow Wilson, his cabinet, and their families; the taboo against this scandalously popular form of entertainment had been dissolved.

And the final sweeping influence that opened up the country physically was the motor car. The common man now had a carriage similar in kind, if not in price, to the carriage of a prince.

At first there was resistance to all these forms of openness. President Wilson, who was given to philosophizing, thought that the automobile would be just another trinket of the rich and powerful. And until Henry Ford came along, he was right. Wilson feared that "nothing has spread socialistic feeling in this country more than the use of the automobile. . . . To the countryman they are a picture of the arrogance of wealth, with all its independence and carelessness." Later, the radio, too, was viewed with alarm by then Secretary of Commerce Herbert Hoover. The controversy raged over whether radio should be allowed to become a commercial device. Hoover thought it was "inconceivable that we should allow so great a service, for news, for entertainment, for educational and for vital commercial purposes to be drowned by advertising chatter."

In my opinion, the essential character of the American spirit prevailed in both cases. The "advertising chatter" became a powerful tool to spread the benefits of the country's production across the land. The "arrogance of wealth" of the motor car became the average man's access to a better life. The open-door policy is an American idea.

# Ten
*

# Laughter, Little Guys, and Fat Ladies

Laughter is the sound people make when they recognize the truth. So why do we laugh at those staples of vaudeville and the silent comedies, the pratfall, the pie in the face, the little tramp with the broken heart who can't do anything right? That's truth? You heard right —it's truth.

When we watch a movie or play, we're transported into the scene. But the scene will mean something to us only if we can identify with the characters, which is to say, only if we *see ourselves* on stage, or on film. So when we laugh at the fat policeman about to step on a banana peel, we're laughing at ourselves, not at Ben Turpin or Lou Costello or Stan Laurel. And when we say to ourselves, "That's how things are!" we are seeing the truth of the episode.

In my theory, such an explanation doesn't mean that every recognition of the truth provokes laughter. It can provoke anger also. But I see anger as a bump and laughter as a hollow, and, as the man said, nothing resembles a bump so much as a hollow.

Laughter and anger are both free, spontaneous, unrehearsed, and uncalculated. I can be angry at a police department operating like the Keystone Cops, but I can find the Keystone Cops funny in any uniform. All this has been said many times before; comedy and tragedy are two masks of the same face. But let me enlarge a bit on what laughter looks like.

Don't you laugh to yourself when you see something you never saw before? Just a little internal chuckle? Laughter needn't be raucous; it can be a nod, or a firm handshake. It can be a Fred Astaire grimace as he realizes the girl he is pursuing has turned her back on him once more. I was always disappointed that there wasn't more laughter in cowboy or adventure films. They were always so deadly serious, for the most part—fascinating, too, to people like me—but I think in retrospect that they didn't say much about reality. And a clue to that is the way they didn't inspire that smile of recognition.

Among the movie greats, Clark Gable comes to mind first as the personification of laughter. He imbued every line of dialogue with that mischievous smirk of recognition of some abiding truth. On the distaff side, Mabel Normand, in her brief career, showed the same quality. Am I a victim of nostalgia? Here's what Gene Fowler said of her in his biography of Mack Sennett, *Father Goose*:

> She was an innate mimic, but could not imitate mental processes. Possibly she was an authentic genius. Perhaps Isadora Duncan was the only other woman of our time to possess beauty, charm, ability, soul, and courage the equal of Mabel's. And, like the gallant Isadora, Mabel walked with tragedy. Mabel had yet another outstanding quality—a Rabelaisian laughter and bludgeoning wit. . . . If there is one thing the self-appointed nincompoops of censorship cannot bear, it is laughter. Mirth is not in their prune-whip brains. Gaiety is not in their flaccid loins. Humor does not flow in their macaroni arteries. They do not understand the spring freshets of laughter, and therefore fear it as a deluge.

And here we come face to face with the paradox of censorship: In seeking to protect us from the dangers of false doctrines and false values, it shelters us from the truth. That's why, in Gene Fowler's terms, the censor is humorless by definition. He can't open himself to the fact that is confirmed by all of history, that what is forbidden takes on the luster of a spurious desirability. I'm not talking about some straw man; there's a censor in all of us.

We don't want to face reality because sometimes we think it will be bad for us. And we go to absurd lengths to conceal the reality from others, thinking that it will obligingly go away through that same effort.

Consider the simple matter of height. A he-man is supposed to be tall in the saddle. If he's a movie star, he's supposed to be larger than life. Granted, our society is shot through with this prejudice; employment agencies routinely report that corporations are more likely to promote the taller man, and this may derive from some distant patterns of our ethology in which, in the fight for survival and the pursuit of mates the taller members of the species came out ahead. All right. But the silver screen all but hand-tints its images to create the illusion of big-star-tall-guy.

When fans first meet Kirk Douglas in person, they are flabbergasted that he isn't a six-footer. His manner is so intense and his portrayals so powerful—and perhaps the cameramen helped, too—that people who have watched him all their lives on the screen picture him as a tall man. Yet he and dozens of other vigorous male leads are *not* tall, and make no bones about their actual measurements, Dustin Hoffman, Al Pacino, Alan Ladd, Mickey Rooney, Edward G. Robinson, to name a few. Once I had a long talk with Billy Rose on this subject, and the diminutive showman laughed, "I'm taller than anybody I know when I stand on my wallet." What is laughable, in the sense in which I'm talking about laughter in this chapter, are the antics some stars go through to preserve the illusion of height.

Few people know about the great battle of the shoes that went on between Humphrey Bogart and George Raft. Raft was a great dancer and a multidimensional actor, but he was bothered by the fact that his tough-guy image was sometimes diminished by the height of his co-stars. In *Souls at Sea* he was paired with gangly Gary Cooper, and had elevated shoes to top all elevated shoes specially made so he could almost match belt buckles with his younger colleague. In a film soon after, Raft had no fears about playing opposite

Humphrey Bogart because he knew he had him topped. In fact, in the opening sequences of *Invisible Stripes*, they appeared together in a shower and Bogie was a good half-inch shorter. In the next scene, however, both men appeared with their clothes and shoes on and, lo and behold, Bogart suddenly had an edge on him. Raft examined his co-star up and down. A smile tugged at Boggie's mouth when he saw Raft see that he was wearing well built-up shoes.

Raft had been outdone that time, but the tables were soon to be turned. Their next picture was the famous *They Drive by Night.*

"It's a good thing nobody noticed how we changed height in that last movie," Raft said good naturedly to Bogart.

"Yeah, we're not growing boys anymore," Bogart answered. But when they went on camera, Raft had put back into service the platforms he had worn with Cooper, and there he proudly stood—again a half-inch taller than his pal.

I don't really know if these two stars took themselves and their height all that seriously in private life; perhaps they only thought it was important for their careers. If not, it's sad. A person has to come to terms with what he is before he can really accomplish much. He has to be able to laugh at least inwardly at his funny nose, his big feet, his raspy voice, his paunch, or whatever minor physical oddities he may have, knowing that if he really thought about it, they wouldn't be oddities at all.

I have to admit, though, it was a long time before I came to terms with my own "oddities." My father was a short man, and so am I, perhaps a little below average in this age of basketball players and all-protein diets. I was self-conscious growing up. Even after I was making a respectable salary working for the likes of Paul Whiteman and Kate Smith and Martin Block, I secretly wished I had the big-man appearance. Then the great man Georgie Price knocked that silliness out of my head. You may remember him as a vaudevillian, but he went on to become a Wall Street stockbroker of some prominence. This all-around guy had been a National Boys billiards champion in his youth. He was a good adviser. He looked *up* at me and said, "If all the rest of the world combined worried as much about how you look as you do, then you'd have something to worry about."

Anything I might have feared about my height has been made up for many times over by casual comments such as this one: "I'd like a bouquet of lilies on my coffee table, that's what I yearn for in the end. Maybe to meet Joe Franklin, to touch him, a real American man." That thought came out of nowhere in an interview by Jan Hodenfield in the *New York Post*; the speaker was singer Peter Wolf, who had recently been in the news with regard to his marriage to Faye Dunaway. I've been called a lot of things, but never a real American man, by someone who ought to know one.

There's no denying that physical differences can cause severe psychological pain. People, especially younger people, can be cruel in their teasing of a fat girl or a skinny boy. My point is that if a person can rise above that kind of sniping, he or she can put it out of mind. In this regard Kate Smith was a model.

In her book, *Upon My Lips a Song*, Kate dwelt at

length on two great embarrassments in her life: the fact that she never married, and the fact that according to some people, her reputation was made on her avoirdupois as much as on her singing. Kate was ahead of her time on both counts. On the first matter, she said, "There is a need for a different attitude on the part of society for the unmarried woman . . . as a perfectly normal person with the same hopes, wishes, and ambitions as anyone. She has merely fulfilled them differently." She took in good humor numerous jokes about her single state, and was especially gracious in not trying to throw mud back at her tormentors in the pose of a feminist defending her rights. Her weight problem was particularly burdensome when she was trying to break into show business. Her first role was that of "Tiny Little" in *Honeymoon Lane* on Broadway. When she got the news that she had landed a part, at first she was ecstatic. Then it dawned on her that it was the role of a buffoon.

"They had told me my weight, then about 190 pounds, would be a handicap to my career, whereas I now had to acknowledge, to my dismay, that it had actually gotten me the part," she writes. Successive roles came her way, too, but they all seemed to be those of the stooge. Fellow actors would go out with her, and "press food on me in an embarrassing manner."

But Kate persisted in her quest for recognition as a performer, not a comedienne. By the time I first met her, in 1947, she had put all that torment so far behind her she could tell stories on herself that made us laugh and cry at the same time. What impressed me most was her advice about fearing rejection. If anyone should have had that fear, it should be Kate, trying to break into Broadway musicals at 190 pounds, but her analysis of the situation is that the fear of rejection is what *causes* most rejections.

Years later, I was trying to put together a show or series of shows featuring all the old dancers from the thirties musicals and movies. George Raft was one of the best I got, even though he seldom went back to dancing after his great *Tango*. And he was available whenever he was in New York. So was Ginger Rogers. I knew that my prize catch would be Ruby Keeler. But I was afraid she would turn me down flat. I was like a bashful boy at the senior prom, burning to ask a beautiful girl for a dance but afraid of the expected brush-off, and the hee-haws from everyone within hearing. Ruby Keeler came down to the Roseland Dance City to receive a golden tap shoes award a few years ago. I was the MC, and here was my chance! Miss Keeler sat backstage all alone throughout the run of *No, No, Nanette*, and told me she was dying for an invitation to come on my TV show.

**We all have handicaps, but we don't have to help them defeat us.** Learning to live with them is one thing; correcting them is another. Would Eddie Cantor have gotten off the ground if he hadn't changed his name from Izzy Iskowitz? I went to high school with an ambitious guy named Bernie Schwartz. (Benjamin Franklin, by the way, was the name of the school—at least *my* name was OK.) He's now fulfilled his first ambition by writing a novel that has caught the eye of the critics. In between those two events, we knew him best by a more promotable name, Tony Curtis. Mack Sennett used to tell the story about the reason for his change of name when he and his brothers went into vaudeville. "What's wrong with Sinott?" his father asked proudly. "Dad, in vaudeville they're not going to let me get away with 'And now, the S'nott Brothers.' "

The man who accompanied Eddie Cantor on the piano when he made his start as a restaurant performer had a handicap of a different sort. That man was Jimmy Durante. And he had a lemon, so he made lemonade.

Jolson had a gimmick, too, but few people know how he came up with his patented kneeling act. He was starring in a musical, *Honeymoon Express*, early in his career, when he came down with a serious ingrown toenail on his left foot. The pain was so intense that he was on the verge of dropping out of the show. Instead, he managed to relieve the pain that fateful night by getting down on one knee halfway through the performance, and pouring out his sentimental ballads with a great show of emotion. He later worked the technique into his famous "My Mammy" number—long after the offending toe had healed. In the short time I knew Jolson, by the way, I found to my delight that he was far from being only the result of these and other gimmicks. Vibrations came from his body—the only case in which I understood what people mean by "good vibes." Joley died in 1950. He was a guest on my "Vaudeville Isn't Dead" radio show in 1949.

**What all these stories tell me is that what is a vexing problem to one person is highly amusing to another**. The idea is to be able to see it from both points of view—whether you're the one who's vexed or amused.

Steve Allen used to do a marvelous routine along these lines. He'd take letters out of the newspaper and simply read them with gusto. The more indignant the letter, the more uproarious the result.

Every now and then something will go wrong in the studio. An engineer will throw a wrong switch or a camera will be on the wrong person, and we'll have to do a segment of the show over. Visitors in the studio invariably look for some kind of outburst from me. Sometimes they ask me after the show why I wasn't angry. I was angry, I assure them, but then I tried to look at it from the point of view of the visitor. *I* am in the position of the man about to slip on the banana peel. *I* am about to get a pie in my face. *I* am the stuffed shirt about to have his hat knocked off by a snowball. And when it happens, the audience should laugh. The joke's on me. But if I can look at it as if I'm both the audience and the performer, I can laugh at my own anger.

The last time I interviewed Jerry Lewis turned out to be just that—the *last* time. Like other talk-show hosts, I had been warned by veteran Lewis watchers—and by the star's staff as well—to stay away from one subject at any cost: Dean Martin, Jerry's partner of old. Unlike other talk-show hosts, however, I ignored the warning.

I wasn't *looking* for trouble, of course; it was simply that as a professional interviewer, someone lucky enough to be earning his living poking his nose into other people's business, I felt I owed it to my viewers to get the most I possibly could out of all my guests. Even sensitive superstars such as Jerry Lewis.

So I went ahead and asked the Telethon King if he had seen his former co-star lately. Just like that, sort of casual-like, if you know what I mean.

It was as if I had pressed some kind of panic button.

"No wonder you're the Nostalgia Nut!" is what Jerry screamed at me. "Don't you read the newspapers? Don't you live on this planet? We broke up over ten years ago!"

Sensing I was already on pretty thin ice, I replied that yes, I did read the papers now and then, and yes, like everyone else on this planet, I knew that Dean and Jerry were not, to put it mildly, on the best of terms. But, I hastily added, I knew that my viewers—and all the Jerry Lewis fans—were understandably curious about whether or not the two entertainers had ever reestablished any sort of contact over the years.

All of which made Jerry even more furious, and for a few terrible seconds I had the feeling my honored guest was on the verge of doing something drastic. Like punching me in the mouth.

I guess I wasn't the only one who had that impression, because when it looked as if Jerry and I were about to make television history, my director, Bob Diamond, faded into a commercial.

I suppose I should have forgotten about the incident long ago, but to this day it somehow bothers me that a man as talented and successful as Jerry Lewis, a man who seemingly has everything in the world going for him, could get so visibly upset over such a simple and natural question as "Have you seen your old pal lately?"

**I look at it this way: Anger can only hurt the angry**

**man**. Those juices that are released when your face gets red can only do *you* harm. If the guy behind you in a traffic jam honks his horn at you, wave to him, or smile. But don't honk back or give him a stern look. That's a jab in your own ribs.

**A final thing that I have learned from little guys and fat ladies: Chance events help you rather than hurt you.** Little gimmicks sometimes add up to a big break. And laughter is the common denominator that helps us recognize the humanity in other human beings. Peter Wolf didn't call me a real American man because I'm a great lover or a reformer. I get mentions in some of the most prestigious columns, for the most obscure reasons, not because I've ever won any awards. There may be a touch of the little tramp in me —which reminds me of this story, again from the fertile pen of Gene Fowler.

Mack Sennett's big leading man, Ford Sterling, was about to quit and go with Mack's cameraman, Pathé Lehrman, into a rival studio. The maestro was brooding with fiancée Mabel Normand over the implications of the move. Then he got a hunch about a replacement for Sterling, thinking back to their days in New York. Fowler reconstructs the moment:

> "Do you remember when we both were at Biograph, and I took you one night to the American Theatre?"
>
> "Sure. In Eighth Avenue. We took a bus ride up Riverside Drive."
>
> "Do you remember the act that impressed us most?"
>
> "Yes, it was pantomime, with a little fellow in a box, watching the show and pretending he was drunk."
>
> . . . Sennett lapsed into silence. Then: "Well, I've

been trying to think of the name of that fellow in the box. I think it was Cunningham or Cantwell or something. I can't remember the darn name, can you?"

"No," Mabel said, "I can't. But I remember the act was presented by Karno's Pantomime Company."

Mack was excited. "That's it. And it all comes back to me now. The manager was Alf Reeves. And the little comedian's name was . . . damn it! I had it on the tip of my tongue. . . . But this chap, what's-his-name, Carlson or Kincaid, has got something."

"He was funny," said Mabel. "There was something kind of sad about him. That's what I remember most. He was sad; he made your heart ache, but he was funny. Don't you remember what I said: 'That guy was born with two strikes on him'? What *was* his name, anyway?"

Sennett telegraphed his agent about the Karno act He described in detail the man he wanted to hire There was a delay. Then a wire came back:

FELLOW'S NAME CHARLIE CHAPLIN STOP HAS FORTY WEEKS SOLID BOOKING STOP WON'T TAKE CHANCE WITH MOVIES STOP

The happy ending, of course, was that Sennett changed Chaplin's mind. This was the man who embodied, as no one before or since, Shelley's lines in "To a Skylark":

We look before and after,
  And pine for what is not:
Our sincerest laughter
  With some pain is fraught;
Our sweetest songs are those that tell of saddest thought.

# Eleven
*

# Today Is a King in Disguise

The here and now is the distillation of all the past and are unbeholden to anything in the future. But what is the here and now? Is it a second, a millisecond? Or is it a moment, that vague word which signifies an aura flowing around a point in time? If you think about it enough, you begin to realize that the present moment isn't anything; it vanishes just as we think about it. Perhaps we're better off not thinking about it, except that so many "thinkers" have told us to prize this moment, this hour, this day, and not dwell in the past or dream about the future.

Ralph Waldo Emerson said, "Write it in your heart that every day is the best day of the year. . . . Today is a king in disguise." I think that's the key to the elusive "here and now." A day is a natural unit in our lives. It's well defined by our friend, the sun. It's a unit we can grasp in our planning without resorting to date books. And it, in turn, is logically divided into units by our various activities—eating, working, traveling, cocktail hour, siesta, coffee break, paper reading, preparing for bed, sleeping. There's the rub. It's so structured for most of us that it carries us along, sometimes unwillingly, almost always unwittingly. It's a puppeteer, and we dangle from the tangle of strings, with seldom an upward glance to the controlling hand.

So I would like to make a suggestion, one of those suggestions that none of us can put into practice for any sustained period, but which at least reminds us of an ideal: **Try to make each day different.** Break up the routine. Experiment with a different lunch hour. Make a new friend. Say something outlandish. Take off that tie. Eat an apple instead of a steak. Remove your blinders to the ordinary things around you. Do an experiment: Listen for sounds, look for sights, or touch things around you that never seem to come to your attention. Make a paper airplane, sketch a familiar face, hum a song you once knew. All these things intensify life, extend time. Psychologists such as Robert Ornstein tell us that our senses are arranged in such a way as to systematically limit and confine our reception of data—light, sound waves, impressions. Our brain tells our eye to see only what is critical for the brain's performance, whose chief function is to keep this machine we call our body *going*. **But life is more than mechanics, so we have to talk back to our brain and tell it we want to see other things, too.** We want to smell flowers as strongly as we smell the garbage truck coming down the street at us. We want to listen to symphonies as well as to sirens.

And what if we could remember every day the way we remember those pivotal days in our life? What if, say, June 21, 1952, was a day about which you could say, "Hmmmm, That's the day I took Margie out to lunch and we talked about her vacation." More likely, there are only a few days in your past that you can fit events to with any accuracy. On my television show guests are invited to reminisce freely, but very seldom do they recall a particular day. The exceptions stand out: Billy Conn and Joe Louis once spent a good half hour talking about the big moments in their boxing careers, and Conn said with a big grin, "I thought I had you, Joe, in the thirteenth." That's to be expected. Another guest recalled the evening he went to a violin concert in a small theater in New Jersey to hear Fritz Kreisler's first performance after returning from the war in Europe. The famed composer had gone back to his native Austria at the outbreak of World War I and enlisted as an ambulance driver. Wounded several times, he was discharged and now here he was, coming on stage to resume his career. But they wouldn't let him play! The applause was so protracted for this heroic, beloved figure that the lights had to be turned out to allow the performance to begin. That's the kind of moment that's easy to remember, since it's so great. How fortunate we would be if we had more than a dozen or so such experiences.

Now, if you ask me what great days I remember, don't expect dates, but I will give you faces and stories. Unfortunately, hearing about them all would be something like watching a four-hour performance on your neighbor's slide viewer after his trip to the Far East. There were many great lines, of course, such as the time Mike Nichols and Elaine May wanted to touch me because I had known Eddie Cantor. "Joe, I know Albert Schweitzer is a great humanitarian," Mike said, "but is it true you *actually knew* Cantor?" I like to tell callers, "Come on by and let's have a sandwich—bring pastrami on rye." And I mean it. As much as I idolize the great moments of the past, boy do I crave the company of good people! If they can take a joke, are satisfied with a sandwich, and don't stand on formality, they'll make my day. And if they want, I'll talk about Cantor.

**What I'm driving at is that if you prize the moment, you will create something to remember. If you smother the moment in idle memories, you're a retread,** the key word being *idle*. Someone once said that the real proof of a woman's courtesy is for her to have an ailment just like the one another woman is describing to her, and not tell her about it. Memories are idle if they're used as a form of one-upmanship. Remember those ailments in your own reveries, and don't burden the conversation with them. On the other hand, don't *hide* your secret ambitions, your ups and downs. I don't mind showing people my rejection slips, my proposals that just gathered dust; I'm collecting those, too.

You know something? Our generation has this unique quality: We're hipped on *today*. It comes, of course, from people like Teddy Roosevelt and Dale Carnegie and Franklin Roosevelt and Billy Graham.

Don't put it down; it's a flavor of enthusiasm that the ancient Greeks tried to stir up, and couldn't quite. It's a vigor that Jack Kennedy loved to talk about, but had taken away from him. He would be in his sixties now, but he has remained eternally young. He knew he was onto something that was new. What Renaissance men, what men of The Enlightenment talked about the here and now? Except for aphorisms, what Greek or Roman poet talked about the little things that make life for the average person worth living?

Social scientists, anthropologists, take note of the new tendency of human beings to look ahead to the future beyond the boundaries of class. In the past, one's chances in the future were all according to social caste. Now, with most social barriers down, all governments are having to contend with the preservation of the race as a whole, not just parts of it.

Some say we're mortgaging our futures for our present enjoyment. True, but we're also balancing the risks by taking out life insurance for our progeny; we're trying to create a system that is far more socially secure than anything that can be established through Social Security Insurance. This is the only bright sign I detect in the spread of credit cards: It's an augury of hope on practical grounds.

**You can't believe in the future unless you believe in the value of the present moment.** Argue that point with yourself. All immorality has been conceived of as trading present pleasure for long-term pleasure. We overeat, regardless of its possible life-shortening effects. We tell tall tales, despite what it may do to our trustworthiness. They tell us that if we were really smart we would place an interest-value on our daily deeds, as if we were investing in stocks and bonds or putting virtue-money in the bank. That's an accountant's view of morality, in my opinion. But life isn't a column of figures. I say that if you strive to do at the moment what the moment promises, and think of the consequences only in the background, you'll do all right.

Did you ever notice how all expressions of the value of today eventually turn to growth, life, nature? "Today, while the blossoms still cling to the vine," the song says. "Give us this day our daily bread," says the universal prayer of Christians. "Today is the first day of the rest of your life." There must be something we're trying to say in all this; I think it's a return to that proposition we started out with: The daily routines of living *are* the values of living. What we do is what we aspire to. **We have to look for the values of the moment in what each moment is, not what it offers.**

Because the revolutions of the earth measure time for us, we have to learn to live within their patterns. Winter, spring, summer, fall. We have to dare mighty events, as Roosevelt said, within these confines. We have to think of building time to the measure provided, in the way we arrange our days. We have to change our daily patterns to open our senses to all that is out there asking to be let into our minds.

Best of all, we don't have to do *anything*. If today is a king in disguise, you are at least his chancellor.

# Twelve
*
# Zest!

Zest is the last thing I will willingly yield when they come to foreclose on my life. Don't worry—I'm not planning anything drastic. The way I talk about the good old days people think I must be doddering. But remember, I was still in my teens when I got my start in radio after the war. The *Second* World War, mind you. So you figure it out. I'm a young man! I'm younger than I think I am. It's zest that does it for you.

Don't ever forget Picasso. They kept bothering him about his age. "How can you be so alert and alive, you old fool?" they were saying, and his answer was, "Age only matters when one is aging. Now that I have arrived at a great age, I might just as well be twenty." He also said something like, "A man is as old as he thinks he is. I think I'm about thirty-two." (Doesn't that remind you of the old W. C. Fields line? You know: "The thing that distinguishes man from the lower animals is man's ability to think. I think I'll have another drink.")

I think I'll have another twenty-five or so. I want to see the year 2000 at any rate. But enough of that. Don't talk about the years ahead or the years behind. Talk about now. Live a day at a time. As Johnny Cash sings, don't be like people who have their heads so set on heavenly things that they're no earthly good. Don't hedge the present for some day in the future. Don't bet on horses—bet on people.

I like what I'm doing so much I overdo it. I prize all the people who make it possible. People call in from nursing homes to tell me how much I brighten their day. I gave a commencement address (OK, it was just an ad-lib talk) at a restaurant school the other day, and they applauded as if I were Julia Child. I'm an honorary member of just about every ethnic organization in town. Nobody has been able to figure out whether I lean to the liberal side or the conservative side, to the Irish or to the blacks—and for a very good reason: I don't lean to either. I especially prize the audiences I'm not expected to attract, such as college kids. They've got zest, and maybe they see it in me. Here's how disc jockey Art Ford described my entry into WNEW almost thirty years ago:

> The way Joe looked when he got inside a studio, you could see he wanted to take the whole thing home with him. The first thing I knew, he was in the music de-

> partment, and the next thing I knew, he was doing his own nostalgia show. In the music department, he worked specifically with Martin Block, who was the greatest d.j.–salesman. It was like being trained by the master.

That first splash of zestiness didn't drop down from heaven, however. You must know that I used to keep notebooks by the radio and try to copy down all the routines of Fred Allen, Jack Benny, Eddie Cantor, Bob Hope, and Ken Murray. Sometimes those shows were on different stations at the same time. I solved that problem by keeping two radios going at once. That's how I learned, by the way, to carry on two telephone conversations at the same time. **Zest is infectious.** it bothers me to see some of the books that come out advising us to play it close to the vest. Some people seem to think that if you know a good thing, you should button your lip—that if your friends are enthusiastic about something, you should play along with them until you can take advantage of them. I disagree. You'll win the battle but lose the war. The war is life itself, not money or prestige or power or sexual domination or the family crest. If zest doesn't come naturally to you and spill out to all your friends, you're kidding yourself; something is wrong somewhere.

Believe me, I've had an informal opinion poll on the subject going for more than twenty-five years, though I didn't have to keep a scorecard. Almost without exception the successful people I've seen on my show have been enthusiastic, open, outgoing, up. They've got zeal and zip. The ones who make life a game of wits and deception sometimes have money, sometimes have power, but you can read the price they're paying for it on their faces. Conversely, many of the most zestful people who have passed through my portals have had troubles of one kind or another. They've had health problems, or bad marriages, or just bad luck. And yet they still have a lust for life that makes me jealous.

Gwen Verdon had a penchant for getting in the middle of stage accidents. But the worse the accident, it seemed, the more successful the performance. She told me about two of her smash hits—

"During *Redhead* an entire set fell on me. It consisted of heavy jail bars and it landed on my feet. Bob Fosse jumped over the orchestra pit to see if I was hurt. The producer of the show ran on stage and yelled, 'Is there a doctor in the house?' Well, it was just my luck to have red hair, and Fosse and the producer had red hair, so the audience thought it was just a natural part of *Redhead*! When they finally carried me offstage five doctors came up from the audience. All of them were psychiatrists!

"In the out-of-town previews of *Damn Yankees*, a fence was moved on stage at the wrong time and smacked me in the side of the head. There I was trying to play voluptuous Lola to Joe Hardy—with blood spouting from my head. I thought it was perspiration, but Joe got sick and had to turn his eyes away. They patched me up at intermission and we staggered through it. Be careful what you say to me about a 'hit' show!"

Like Gwen, most of my favorites in this business have been exuberant about life despite a lot of turmoil and trouble throughout their careers: Jolson, Cantor, Kovacs are obvious examples. Zest, in some cases, may very well be a reaction to adversity. I don't pretend to know if you're born enthusiastic or not; but I do know you can "catch on" if you want to. It's something like making mayonnaise (my mother told me—I'm no chef): All it takes is that first little drop of oil to jell, and presto! You've got mayonnaise. All the oil in the world won't help you if the first drop doesn't catch on. Here are some ideas for getting zest into your life.

**Look for the funny side of things.** Don't practice lugubriousness. Practice laughing. Ally yourself with funny people. Walk away from bitchy, cynical talk. Sure, there are tragedies all around us. As a rule, good things should be *talked about* and bad things should be *acted on*. As I said, laughter is the sound we make when we recognize the truth; the truth is that life is full of hope and excitement and surprises. If you have to read elegies and somber things, do it as a mad fling from your steady diet of good humor.

**Make a conscious effort to do something for nothing.** This is in line with the first suggestion here. Be friendly to people you don't like very much, pay more than your share of the lunch, give a tip when you don't have to, smile at children even when you're in a hurry. I can hear the disbelievers now! Humbug! Wishful thinking, Joe! Listen, I'm not trying to sell you a bag of philosophy. I'm only telling you what seems to work for me.

As I said at the beginning, I'm privileged to be a sucker. Luck has gone my way. I have enough money and enough standing in my work so that I don't have to be possessive of things. I can take more insults because I'm pretty sure of where I stand with people. All the same, others who aren't so lucky as I am make it a habit of doing something for nothing, too. They work with kids who are suspicious of adults. They volunteer their time washing dishes when the other guests are whooping it up. Their reward is zest.

**Don't be jealous of the other guy's success.** That's a general rule that comes as no surprise; the important part is, *show* you're not envious. Don't stint in sharing someone else's joy. That old cynic, Ambrose Bierce, was tough on women on the subject of jealousy; "When Eve saw her reflection in a pool, she sought Adam and accused him of infidelity." But men also are apt to be envious at the drop of a hat, or the drop of a salary figure. The point is, you can learn how to be joyful by sharing someone else's good news.

When the transcontinental railroad was finally completed at Promontory Point, Utah, in 1869, the event was hailed as the best news of the century up to that time. In a poem titled "What the Engines Said," Bret Harte wrote of the two engines that met to break each other's bottle of champagne:

> What was it the Engines said,
> Pilots touching—head to head
> Facing on a single track,
> Half a world behind each back?
> . . . . . . . . . . . . . . . . . . . . . . . . . . . . . . . . . . . . . . . . . . . . . . .
> You brag of the East! *You* do?
> Why *I* bring the East to *you*!
> All the Orient, all Cathay,
> Find through me the shortest way;
> and the sun you follow here
> Rises in my hemisphere.

That's a fair sample of the exuberance of those days, especially in writers like Harte and Twain. The West was conquered by men with an unbounded enthusiasm for living. What was the advertisement that called for Pony Express riders? Long hours, grueling labor, poor food, chances for survival uncertain—but adventure! In 1848, when the news of the discovery of gold flashed across the country from California, the difficulty of traversing the country was a favorite subject of cynics. The *New York Herald* dismissed the idea of extending the railroads to the goldfields: "This whole project is ridiculous and absurd. . . . Centuries hence it will be time enough to talk of such a railroad." Yet in just twenty-one years that railroad was a reality.

Something has gone out of our lives with the passing of this symbol of the youth of America. Young boys will no longer grow up with the call of the locomotive's whistle in their ears. Yes, there are still passenger trains, but they're a grudging concession. Back then, the tracks said "West" to a boy in a small Midwestern town. They said "Big city" to the farm boy. They were in the bloodstream of Whitman and Sandburg; what's in the bloodstream of Bellow and Ginsberg?

Zest also means looking at what is all around us. I would like to see people travel less and see more. I would like them to see more of their neighbors. I would like to see children holding on longer to their sense of wonder. I would like to see old people welcomed back into society.

Whenever I visit a nursing home, to give an award or just to entertain, I am struck by the will of old people to *belong*. Their loneliness is such a delicate thing; it can slip into despair so easily. When will we realize that their minds are open for us, their imaginations are still full, their wisdom is a part of the humanity of us all?

Ernest Hemingway prefaced *For Whom the Bell Tolls* with John Donne's poem, the source of his title. He used Donne's original spelling and underscores, and also the original placement of the text on the page, with the last six lines tapering to a point, where his name was placed—

No man is an Iland, intire of it selfe; every man
is a peece of the Continent, a part of the maine; if
Clod bee washed away by the Sea, Europe is the lesse,
as well as if a Promontorie were, as well as if a Mannor
of thy friends or of thine owne were; any mans
death diminishes me, because I am involved in Mankinde; And therefore
never send to know for
whom the bell tolls; It
tolls for thee.
JOHN DONNE

The loneliness of one down-and-outer on Forty-second Street, or of one helpless grandmother in a wheelchair, or of one child adrift in the ghetto diminishes the humanity of us all. Our zest for life, no matter how insignificant that life may seem, is the saving grace of humanity.

# Thirteen
# *
# Messages

Millions of people look in the mail each day for good news. The mailbox is the hope chest of America. It's also a symbol of what we all want in life: personal exchange. I'm being rather didactic about this, but see if it isn't part of the truth.

I know I look forward to the mail delivery, even though it's full of what we call junk mail. It's not junk! Maybe the people who send it should be charged more, just to help them sharpen their approach. But it carries information, and I know a lot of people who would love to have any kind of mail, junk or otherwise. The people who look for mail the most are those who don't get other kinds of messages. That's what we all want—*messages*.

I look for telephone messages. I get nervous when the phone doesn't ring. I think you get nervous when you don't receive the messages you are accustomed to receiving. And I think the people I talk to on the phone and in my office are no different. That's why I cater to them. Even to the point of looking foolish to bystanders.

A young man of great promise, and greater girth, has been hanging around my place for some time, looking for news and encouragement about a special project of his, which, in my opinion, at least, is a long shot. He's a jovial fellow, and I thought I had sensed his "laughter quotient" in watching him react to the typical conversation in the office. So when he was about to leave one night recently, I didn't hesitate to have a laugh at his expense. He dropped a pencil on the floor as he wrested himself from his chair. I said to Pop, "pick up that pencil. And Jack, whatever you do, don't bend over."

As he went out the door, he offered a ride to a young writer from Berkeley, California, who was nervous about getting back to his place on the Upper East Side at midnight on a Saturday by subway. The man of course accepted; they knew each other better for having been audience to a paltry bit of humor. Having no audience left, I said to Pop, with feeling, "God *bless* him, he's fat!"

The subject is messages—how we send them out, how they're received, and especially why more should be sent out even if we're not sure how they're received. **My practice is, if there is any doubt at all, send a message to dispel that doubt.** Even a mildly discouraging message is better than doubt. And so I don't temper my tongue unless I am certain my listener is a hypochondriac. Here are some examples, pretty much at random:

Late one evening a young protégée called, without much to say. I had to delay a moment to remember what my connection with her was. Then I remembered, and said, "You were a smash. Everybody in town is talking about the show. And you know something? You did it all yourself. How many hours did you spend working for that moment? I'm so *proud* of you. Made about fifty dollars, huh? That's good. That's better than you think. You know something? With all the friends in the world your best friend is yourself. And that fifty dollars means more to you than to anybody. Am I right, sweetheart? God bless you! You know you need friends to confide in and to talk to and to boost you up. But listen to me now. You've gotta boost yourself up, too. You've gotta talk to yourself like nobody else can. Thanks, thanks. Dream on it for me, baby. OK? What a day! What a day. Keep callin' now, right?"

She couldn't get that from her friends, I'm sorry to report. Or maybe her friends were too "realistic," which means they judged her aspirations from their own point of view.

The only reason I think I'm such a great judge of what other people need is that I have failed miserably in my own housekeeping. Apparently, that's in the nature of advice givers. I tried for years, for instance, to get Hedy Lamarr as an anchorwoman on the show, to work with me from time to time in interviewing guests. What perspective she would have given. But I couldn't make the right approach. To everyone else, I would say, "Be direct!" But I myself waited, and waited, and hoped.

And when actress Betty Hutton was given a benefit performance at the Riverboat Restaurant, I was the very fortunate master of ceremonies. Here was another magnificent lady I had admired from afar. I cried at her plight. I did my job that evening, and I listened to what everybody else had to say about the one-time "incendiary blonde." My remarks were quoted in the next day's *New York Times*: "This great star, Betty Hutton, was so busy making movies she didn't arrange for someone to manage her finances. Garbo, Dietrich, Crawford . . . they had advisors. Hutton didn't." Then someone reminded me that I've never had anyone to manage my affairs, either.

Now let me give some advice that I know is part of me. I've said it before at the start of this book, but here it has a different aspect. **If you get in the habit of giving a certain kind of message to other people, pretty soon you're going to give that same message to yourself.** If you always tell friends to be careful, go slowly, look before you leap, you're going to become overly cautious yourself; that is, if you get in the habit of saying no to others all the time, you'll soon start saying no to yourself. The way the logic goes is, "No, you can't do it; therefore, no, *I* can't do it."

Don't confuse this with being assertive. A spate of books recently proclaimed, especially to women, I suppose, that we should learn to say no. To stand up for our real wishes. But to me, that isn't really saying no. If you want to go to Spain and paint for a year and everybody else is telling you it's foolish and dangerous and not what it's cracked up to be but you still truly want to do it, you're not saying no to them, you're saying yes to yourself. That's one of those verbal contortions that logicians have been gabbing about for centuries. A sentence isn't negative just because it has the word *no* in it. And it isn't necessarily positive if the usual negative words aren't apparent. "You're a loser and you always will be!" is about the strongest negative sentence I can imagine.

Isn't being assertive a matter of belief? To do what you want to do, against all the nay-sayers, is to have confidence in yourself. And you can't afford to water down your belief in yourself by believing in too many other things at the same time. On this subject Lewis Carroll had a delightful story to tell, in a letter to a childhood friend, Mary Macdonald—

> Don't be in such a hurry to believe next time—I'll tell you why. If you set to work to believe everything, you will tire out the muscles of your mind, and then you won't be able to believe the simplest true things. Only last week a friend of mine set to work to believe Jack-the-giant-killer. He managed to do it, but he was so exhausted by it that when I told him it was raining (which was true) he *couldn't* believe it, but rushed out into the street without his hat or umbrella, the consequence of which was his hair got seriously damp, and one curl didn't recover its right shape for nearly two days.

**The person who believes everything believes nothing.** But the first thing you must believe is yourself.

Trust your emotions. Trust your feelings about people. Then let that confidence shine out. Don't be afraid to give all of yourself to others, all the confidence and enthusiasm you have inside yourself. Ralph Waldo Emerson said in his memoirs that once early in his teaching career he was worried that if he gave out too much to his students he would be exhausted by the end of the day. But then he discovered that "the more I gave, the more I had to give." That's one of the more remarkable ideas I have come across, and it rings true to me because I see it every day in my own little office. So send out those messages and more will grow inside you, as long as there is a fountain of belief welling up inside you. Messages, after all, come from *someone;* an anonymous message is not only puzzling, but frightening. And the meaning of a message depends heavily on who it comes from. I need not remind you that "I love you" depends for its effect entirely on who the "I" is.

Philosophical wisdom means more to us if we know the speaker. **And a message that comes down to us from the ages gains in meaning if someone we know repeats it with approbation.** Novelists love this trick: They cull the wisdom of the Bible, or Socrates, or Maimonides, and pass it along to us thinly disguised, and we think it's new and vital. Writers especially like to add luster to their work with titles snatched from the immortal prose of the ancients. "Seize the day" was a Greek aphorism that was losing some of its effect when along came Saul Bellow to revive it. Those of us who have read the King James Bible all our lives began to see another world when we heard the line "All creatures great and small, all things bright and beautiful" once again from a Scottish veterinarian with a great, earthy sense of story telling. And sometimes a line loses its forcefulness when we discover it was written by an imposter or second-rate pundit. In Mr. Herriot's case, I think the original message was enhanced.

It's the same in poetry, especially the modern sort that requires such hard work to read and understand. I myself am an admirer of the simple poetry, such as the works of A. E. Housman—simple to read, at any rate. Some of his lines are so simple, in fact, that if taken out of context and read to someone who doesn't know who the poet is, they fall flat. In the fifty-seventh poem in *A Shropshire Lad,* for example, the line "But better late than never" appears. Couldn't he have done better than using that trite old saw, you might ask. On the other hand, the following breezy poem was written more than seventy years ago by a long-forgotten writer of children's poetry. What if we were told its author was T. S. Eliot? He has written a lot of whimsical stuff, you know, such as his book about cats. Would you read more into this than into a nursery rhyme if you knew where the message came from?

*The Town of Don't You Worry*

There's a town called Don't You Worry
On the banks of River Smile,
Where the Cheer-up and Be-happy
Blossom sweetly all the while;
Where the Never-grumble flower
Blooms beside the fragrant Try,
and the Ne'er-give-up and Patience
Point their faces to the sky.

Rustic benches quite enticing
You'll find scattered here and there;
And to each vine is clinging
Called the Frequent-earnest prayer.
Everybody there is happy
And is singing all the while,
In the town of Don't You Worry
On the banks of River Smile.

Certainly, it's corny. It doesn't have the playfulness or the precision of Emily Dickinson. It's just a ditty. But it would be better known, I feel, if we knew who wrote it, and perhaps why.

One of the reasons I like to have someone with me, even walking down the street, is that I want to have someone to send messages to. It's difficult to appreciate a message without knowing the one who is sending it; it's even more difficult to send out messages without knowing who is going to receive them. The poets and playwrights sometimes say they could write even if no one was there to listen, and Miss Dickinson even compared her song to a bird's. In jest she admonished a sparrow outside her window to stop warbling because no one could hear it. But surely seeing the effect of your message on someone else has a lot to do with your continuing to speak.

One of Mahatma Gandhi's most famous messages was an extemporaneous radio broadcast from London in 1931. It carried greater impact than many of his more dramatic pleas because it was addressed to a new audience: America. This and other early radio broadcasts by politicians and reformers changed the medium from a plaything into a powerful social tool. An interesting aside to the story is that the broadcast as heard in America contained two typical bloopers that were common in the early days of radio. Not realizing the mike was on, Gandhi began by saying, "Do I have to talk into that thing?" and at the end, when the engineers waved to him to speed it up and conclude, he gave a heavy sigh of relief, "Well, that's over." Just for the record, here are some of the things he said, speaking without notes of any kind:

> If India is to revive the glory of her ancient past, she can only do so when she attains her freedom. The reason for the struggle having drawn the attention of the world I know does not lie in the fact that we Indians are fighting for our liberty, but in the fact that the means adopted by us for attaining that liberty are unique and, as far as history shows us, have not been adopted by any other people of whom we have record. The means adopted are not violence, not bloodshed, not diplomacy as one understands it nowadays, but they are purely and simply truth and non-violence. Hitherto, nations have fought in the manner of the brute. They have wreaked vengeance upon those whom they have considered to be their enemies. We find in searching national anthems adopted by great nations that they contain imprecations upon the so-called enemy. They have vowed destruction and have not hesitated to take the name of God and seek divine assistance for the destruction of the enemy. We in India have endeavored to reverse the process. We feel that the law that governs brute creation is not the law that should guide the human race. . . . I feel in the innermost recesses of my heart, after a political experience of close upon thirty-five years, that the world is sick unto death of blood-

> spilling. . . . I have therefore no hesitation whatsoever in inviting all the great nations of the world to give their hearty cooperation to India in her mighty struggle.

That message went around the world, but the world heard only part of it. How many times will that message have to be repeated before governments *believe* it?

**I'm beginning to think that the total volume of messages we receive today is diluting what is said.** Many people point the finger at advertising, but I think advertising is just a scrap of paper riding along on the crest of a wave that is much more threatening. There is so much to listen to, to read, to watch, to feel that we find it difficult to channel our thoughts into something constructive. What should we see tonight? What sports event is in the news? Did you catch that new bestseller? You're not aware of that wild new underground magazine? My advice may seem old-fashioned, but give it a hearing: **When in doubt, cherish the personal messages.** If you have a choice between listening to the woman over the back fence who is just an old gossip, or watching a million-dollar-a-year newscaster who has a first-rate mind, go outdoors. To the back fence.

# Fourteen

*

# People Think That Way

People are logical, to be sure, but they have different logics for different situations. That's right—*logics*. What we usually think of as logic is just the mathematical kind, the abstract formulations that the ancient Greeks started. But reasoning and just plain thinking take more forms than just the syllogism.

I overheard a conversation the other day between a husband and wife that went something like this:

HE: Did you buy that record album for me today?

SHE: No, I stayed home all day.

HE: Oh, you didn't go to the store, uh?

SHE: If I stayed home all day how in hell could I go to the store, silly?

HE: Wait a second, honey—I was just—

SHE: Don't you ever listen to me? What kind of an imbecile do you think I am?

HE: Look, it was just idle conversation—

SHE: You never talk to me! That's the trouble. All you have to say to me is idle conversation.

And so on into the night. The woman was completely logical—in the Aristotelian sense. She couldn't be at home all day and also in a store for part of the day. The man exhibited a certain logic, too. You might call it conversational logic. He confirmed with a statement what he already knew by abstract reasoning to be a fact. He was following an ancient rule of conversational expertise: Flow is more important than deductive thinking. If we paused to think about the implications of every piece of dialogue, our talking would be jerky and unnatural.

Of course, it's true that people sometimes violate rules of abstract logic, or, as they say, commit fallacies, yet I've found that, even if they can't give you an example of a syllogism, people usually think pretty straight. (Even college professors usually bungle syllogisms, so don't feel out of step.)

Conversational logic offers the opportunity not only to violate abstract logic, but to add excess baggage to it. It's one thing to go along with this kind of conversation (The same kind that got the *He* in the previous exchange into trouble):

AGENT: How old is that singer?

ME: She's thirty-two.

AGENT: Oh, she's not under thirty, uh?

(In that brief exchange we learn that the agent expected the singer to be younger and may even require that any new talent he represents be under thirty.) It's quite another thing to understand the implications of—

AGENT: Is your singer a young gal?
ME: Al, she's young, she's young. She's under thirty. She's thirty-two.

Here, I'm implying that she acts and looks like a younger person. I'm also saying that I'm pleading a case for her; I don't want chronological age to be a barrier. Perhaps I'm also making an unintentional "funny" that will ease the relationship between the agent and me. All this is conversational logic and it's all legitimate.

There's a little-known story about Joe Louis that I tell occasionally to show what self-control he had. I'll tell it now for another reason. He and the late G.I. comedian, Harvey Stone, were on tour entertaining the troops during the Second World War, and in their uniforms they often went unnoticed by civilians. In New York City one day they were rushing to a performance when the Brown Bomber accidentally sideswiped a cab. The irate taxi driver made tracks to Joe's open window and began hurling abuse on him that covered every racial slur in the book. As the heavyweight champ of the world took it all in, the driver challenged him to a fight, uniform or no uniform. But Joe kept his cool and soon the frustrated cabbie drove off. Stone was flabbergasted. "Joe, why didn't you take at least one tiny swing at him, for all that maligning?" Joe replied, "If someone insulted Enrico Caruso, would he have sung him an aria?"

If you gave that one to a logician, he'd have to say that Joe's premise that a person doesn't respond to an insult in his long suit was false. Right, Harvey? Wrong. If hearts are led, you have to follow suit if you have a heart. If you're challenged to a fight, you have to fight. If you're challenged to a sing-off, you sing. Card games are logical, but life isn't, a lot of the time. That's why Joe's apparent illogic had a logic of its own. He was saying this: I've got an art of my own, like a singer's. I don't have to mix my art with everyday squabbles any more than a singer has to. Right?

I bring all this up in defense of my supposedly illogical method of directing a conversation. You see, I don't think that a conversation has to be geometrically sound. I don't think it has to proceed relentlessly to some conclusion. **In short, I don't think most people look for proof in conversation. They look for interest, for insight, for diversion.** They leave proof for editorials. If you don't believe me, you should tape a cocktail-party conversation someday. Or a husband–wife argument. Or a press conference by an economist.

Sure, I sometimes beat around the bush. But I always look for an answer, not a showdown. I don't think people should talk to each other like Perry Masons or F. Lee Baileys in the courtroom. The last thing I want is a banal dead end, and the next to the last thing I want is an obvious question that can only lead to an obvious answer. Good conversations race along as much on what is left unsaid as on what is said. Oliver Wendell Holmes put it this way—

> The whole force of conversation depends on how much you can take for granted. Vulgar chessplayers have to play their game out; nothing short of the brutality of an actual checkmate satisfies their dull apprehensions. But look at two masters of that noble game! White stands well enough, so far as I can see; but Red says, Mate in six moves—White nods, looks, nods—the game is over. Just so in talking with first-rate men; especially when they are good-natured and expansive, as they are apt to be at table.

**The human mind jumps around unpredictably, but not necessarily disconnectedly.** It makes broad leaps not easily explained by syllogisms, and the elisions aren't always reconstructable. For spoken language is at the very least *words*. It's longing in the eyes, it's an occasional inaudible grunt, it's shifting of feet.

Ralph Waldo Emerson was the butt of many jokes because his essays were so disjointed. It was laughingly said that one could start with the last sentence of one of them as well as the first. Lowell retorted: Did they say he was disconnected? So are the stars.

Oh, yes, sometimes I am Mrs. Malaprop and Sam Goldwyn combined. (Sam, you may recall, was supposed to have a penchant for mixed metaphors.) But I hope I can say till the end of my days that I never do it with evil intent or out of laziness. **My first rule in speaking is never to hurt; my second is never to fake it.** How many times have you heard an interviewer say, "Bill, I breezed through your book and loved it, but I'm not much of a reader, ha ha. Why don't *you* tell us about it?" The truth is that just before the show he told the author he hadn't had time to look at it at all. Now if *I* don't, I ask someone who knows the subject and whose opinions I trust. And that's all I bring up. I don't pretend to have read something when I haven't.

Once Crosby said that Rosemary Clooney could remember all kinds of obscure songs, and run through them on a moment's notice without a slip. I agreed. "She's got a photogenic mind for lyrics," I said, and then laughed at my boner.

I well remember the time I had forgotten that a new commercial was supposed to be read on one of my radio shows. When the moment came to launch into my sales talk, my son Brad, who was writing ads for me at the time, waved at me frantically and started scribbling on a pad. "New ad," he wrote, and he proceeded to block the thing out word by word from his notes. I hemmed and hawed for a few seconds, and then, as I saw he was moving down the page rapidly, I started reading it. But I hadn't timed it well enough. Soon I was running only a word or two behind him, and I got slower and slower. Finally, as I came to the client's name and address, I was so trapped in my pattern that I read it off equally slowly, even though I knew the advertiser's name like my mother's. My audience must've thought it was a taped message and the machine had broken down.

One of the great crimes of television is allegiance to the clock or to some other preconceived idea of the pace and direction of the show. I shudder whenever I'm forced to end an interview prematurely. You can well imagine that it's difficult at times to know if two minutes or ten minutes is enough to cover some aspect of a conversation. Psychologist Rollo May, in *The Cour-*

*age to Create,* said, "In the several times I have been on television, I have been struck by this feeling. . . . Whenever I got an original idea, whenever in these programs I began to struggle with some unformed new concept, whenever I had an original thought that might cross some frontier of the discussion, at that point I was cut off." People watching a show, I suspect, feel the same way. People like to pursue things to some conclusion, logical or not.

Another interesting aspect of conversational logic is how we can adjust it to the medium of exchange. Talking to someone on the telephone is obviously different from talking in person. ("Obviously," I say, but there are also cases in which the other person *doesn't* adjust to the medium. Some people are afraid of the telephone. Some people have such an active imagination they think everything said on a TV show is aimed at them. Some people are so aware of how the author wrote the book that they can't throw themselves into the story. They're technique conscious.)

In general, we convey things by sight or by sound or by sense, or by any combination of the three. The message of a book is conveyed only by its sense (even though it usually takes eyes to read it). A telephone conversation is conveyed by sound, and usually by sense (a lot of people talk only to hear the sound of their voices). Many watch baseball games on TV with the sound turned off, because TV announcers think they have to fill every available moment with talk. There's a different logic to the conversations in each of these cases. Look what I can say to people over the phone:

To a caller who won't listen: "What are you, a man

or a lady?" (He or she answers matter-of-factly, confirming my worst fears. So I say good-bye.)

To a guy who's in the dumps because he can't pay his bills: "No, you're not behind in the rent—the landlord's behind. Don't forget one thing: Being broke is nothing to be embarrassed about—it's only a temporary inconvenience."

To a singer who wants to know if she should take an engagement: "What's it pay, sweetheart? No, never work for nothing. Never. But when you get paid, give them more than their money's worth. That's how you get ahead."

To someone who persists in trying to find out if I've read his book: "I must've read it—I took it home." (That's the logic of a conversation that defies Aristotle. The hidden premise is, "Everything I take home I read." But my caller isn't going to ask me. "Do you read everything you take home?" He gets the message.)

In all these cases, my telephone manner couldn't be duplicated in person or on TV. The phone removes the elements of gestures and distractions, and yet it's far more personal than talking to someone via TV.

I like the telephone especially in trying to give advice. I like it especially for its rifle effect, as opposed to the shotgun blast. When I want to talk personally to someone in the office, I have to wait for a chance to be alone with him. I'll walk him to the elevator, or send him down the hall to a deserted office, until I have a chance to get away. If I said the following to a friend in exactly the same words on the telephone, in person, and in a letter, how different the effect would be:

"How ya doin'? Drinking a little? Don't get back in that rut, will ya? You're my boy!"

So what? So think of your listener before you choose your avenue of communication. Think of how *his* mind works. Think of what he sees in certain charged words. Sound obvious? I know an executive who treats good news and bad news as if they were just *news* to his listeners. One day he called a salesman to request the pleasure of his company in his office. The salesman hopped right over, expecting to work out the details of a deal he had presented. The executive kept him waiting in his outer office, then had him escorted in to inform him in person that he didn't think it was a good idea. He thought that was being personal!

There's a poem I remember from school days that makes the point even better. Actually, I don't remember it; I copied it down in a notebook. (Does your family collect favorite things in notebooks? Vachel Lindsay was a favorite in our home).

*Euclid*

Old Euclid drew a circle
On a sand-beach long ago.
He bounded and enclosed it
With angles thus and so.
His set of solemn graybeards
Nodded and argued much
Of arc and of circumference,
Diameter and such.
A silent child stood by them
From morning until noon
Because they drew such charming
Round pictures of the moon.

# Fifteen

*

# Sweet Harmony

So many people have told me, so many poets proclaim it, so many dancers and singers live it, that I can't listen to those few who would have us believe there is a higher goal than harmony. Sweet, sweet harmony. Remember, I said *goal.* Always in the background is conflict; that's our lot as human beings. Without the ear's memory of dissonance and suspended minor chords the final resolving harmonic would only be another bunch of notes.

Why, then, do many broadcast interviewers feel that they must provoke anger or disagreement in their guests? Do they think anyone worth interviewing is so secretive that he won't reveal anything of himself unless he is challenged? Are they so afraid of being bland that they think only turmoil will do? Whatever the reason, they seek interest in trouble. But would you ask your next-door neighbor if he suspects his wife is sleeping around, or your clergyman if he has ever taken a bribe? Honest, that's what some hosts ask on TV.

**The urge to be sensational is leaking out of the talk-show studios into the newsrooms.** It's no accident that news reports are now shows, and are conducted by teams who gab with each other about the day's events. It's a formula that talk shows perfected. Some call it "happy talk," but I think it's just plain gossip. If you want real news you have to read the newspaper. News is a mixed bag, so you ought to be able to read about what you want to, at your own pace, in depth or in brief, and know who's writing it. When all of America gets a fifteen-minute dose of what someone in New York thinks is entertaining news, and nothing more, then we'll be in trouble. Fortunately, I don't think that will happen. There are too many intelligent people around, both on the transmitting end and on the receiving end.

The great New York adman, George L. Miller, used to write a provocative column in the long-gone *Printer's Ink.* His pen name was Aesop Glim, the last name being concocted from his initials plus *i,* which he said was simply "me." But the Aesop part of it should tell you that his writing was provocative without being obtrusive or nasty. If he criticized someone, and his job in that column was to critique his peers, he did it grandly and with the flair of Horowitz straightening the chair of his Steinway. Once he told me that he didn't want to dwell on anything that disturbed him. He would walk a block out of his way to avoid a certain part of Fifty-third Street that resurrected a memory of an unhappy love affair. But this doesn't mean he was afraid to face life, just that "enough life will face me without me having to search for it." If only he were around today he would be an excellent foil for our quip-happy newscasters.

Way back when I was first starting out in this business, Miller was talking about the great power that television would exert over his business and, by the same token, over all our lives. He believed that people are motivated more by hope than by fear; that the fear of having bad breath was small compared with the hope of attracting that snappy new girl down the street. So he preached harmony as the *end* of everything we do. Even in writing sentences, he said, put the good news last. End on the harmonic chord. After it has gone through its infancy and adolescence, he predicted, TV will turn from violence and sensationalism as the theater and the movies and radio did before it. **People want the good guys to win, they want the boy to get the girl, they want the sun to continue rising.**

He made a prediction that leads me to believe his guesswork is pretty good. He wrote that whenever things seem impossible, when the outlook is bleak and the crisis seems to be the final, overwhelming crisis, something will happen to bring about a happy ending. When New York was becoming so overrun with horses that the subways smelled like a meadow in spring by comparison, along came the automobile. And when the fumes of the internal-combustion engine begin to choke us, a new invention will enter stage left to rescue us. He used to claim that the telephone was invented just to save his life. As he neared retirement age, he longed to resettle in Jamaica. But he had to keep his ad agency going in New York. His clients told him it couldn't be done—an expression, by the way, which should be stricken from your lexicon. But he hired himself an alter-ego to handle his affairs in New York, and conversed daily with everyone he had to—by telephone.

The telephone is, as you have surmised, my weapon and my toy. I like to hear people say good things about this instrument of mediation, this mender of strained relations and soother of lonely hearts. Who said you can't be in two places at once? Thorstein Veblen said that the telephone forced people to talk more than they ever had before in history—a good thing, in my book, though I don't suppose anyone has found a way to measure how much the Romans used to talk. Psychologists seem to be running out of things to study, so I'll suggest this. Why not gather statistics on how many words are uttered in two different cities in a single day, given the same population in each, with half as many telephones in one city as in the other? Added challenge: How many words are uttered in each *not* into the telephone? In short, what has the availability of this magic distance-shortener done to the general conversational habits of people?

If, as Tennyson said, the noblest end of man's labors is to produce a satisfying conversation, the telephone should receive a special Nobel prize. **The telephone**

**companies of the country are our friends.** Oh, they do dreadful things! They ask for deposits, and they cut off our service when the check we say is in the mail isn't. When the phone refuses to give us back our last coin—as a result of which we miss a train and are threatened with divorce—they send us a check for a dime. When we can't get a straight answer from the operator, they refer us to that last resort, the supervisor, and they talk to us as if they are recordings made at a central casting office. But they are our friends if we only knew them.

My son Brad knows how to talk to them. When my phones break down because someone has dropped the receiver on the floor once too often, I ask him to intercede for me with the telephone company. They're busy people, you know. Phones are breaking down all over town, it would seem. So he tells them how my very life depends on having at least two phones, and they are considerate. You must treat the telephone people as if they are honest, hard-working, feeling people. You should visit them at their office from time to time to assure yourself that they are flesh and blood. They really are of the human species, just like you and me.

Sweet harmony doesn't come just from wishing it—we've got to do a million little things all the time to adjust our lives and our attitudes toward making peace with others. The telephone is a wonder (I don't pretend to know anything about how it works, just as I don't know the first thing about the mechanics of a microphone or the electronics of a TV set), yet it brings new demands on our lives along with it. In fact, it's a good example of the risk-benefit process that is the very stuff of our existence.

When the social critic Arnold Bennett toured the United States in the early 1900s, he concluded that all the accomplishments of the inventiveness of this promised land, the proudest and most practical was the telephone. He added, "What startles and frightens the backward Europeans in the United States is the efficiency and fearful universality of the telephone." Today our social scientists and newspaper pundits decry the reign of this terror. Our teenage daughters seem to talk a novel a day on the phone, its ringing interrupts most dinners, and salesmen seem to believe that (1) they have first preference, and (2) they can address you like a long-lost friend, for the price of a phone call. That's part of the risk; think of the benefit. Our job is to reduce the risk.

When someone calls me at my office, I know there must be a little fearfulness that he or she will say the wrong thing, be put off, or be let down. I try to avoid all three possibilities. It may sound dreary in print, but here's a sample of a typical conversation:

"It's so *good* to hear your voice. So good. Are you having a bad day, sweetheart? Take your tranquilizers? You're such a good baby. Now, concentrate on your music. That's right, you've got it. Don't ever give up. Now call me soon. I must hear from you, right?"

OK. That's the soothing part of it. **Harmony also consists in keeping your ego in check.** Curb it like you curb your dog. Carol Pearce once asked me, in a formal interview for publication, "Why did you get the outstanding social critic of the year award, Joe?" I'm dying to tell you all about it. I can be proud in front of you, can't I? But to keep the conversation moving harmoniously, I had to say to Carol, "Where did you hear about that?" Honest, we had more important things to discuss.

I'll match issues with anybody, and I want you to know that I can be irascible about certain issues and certain people. I'm not all syrup and puffed wheat. Just for the record, I think I started this whole business of using the airwaves for serious commentary. At least I don't remember any precedent for the time I put Eddie Cantor on my radio show to talk about a rash of bombings of synagogues. What a response we got! In a few days we raised a relief fund that no one had ever thought possible without a concert at Carnegie Hall. I knew, of course, that Cantor was no newcomer to this subject. In the thirties he had used his popularity to call attention to what Hitler was doing in Germany. Sadly, the radio brass of the time hauled him off the air for being political. And before that he was dropped by Ziegfeld, when Mr. Ziegfeld was king of Broadway, for backing an actors' strike—which, by the way, was the birth of Actors' Equity. Cantor a song-and dance funny man? Sure, but a bigger man than I've seen since in this business.

I'm rather proud of what we've said on the show about air pollution, the need for prison reform, and women's rights, to mention three topics I have dramatized repeatedly—and long before they hit the front pages. I knew I'd always had a large female audience. Abe Margolies, co-producer of *I'm Solomon, Mahagonny,* and *A Joyful Noise,* once said, "Joe can definitely help you on Broadway. Joe hits the women, and they drag the men to see the show. He's got quite an audience. You'd figure that at one o'clock in the morning it's a lost cause. But the last time I was on with Joe, I bet I got a hundred calls about it." What you can do for Broadway you can do for Main Street.

I've had Senator Edward Kennedy on the show many times, but it never crossed my mind to ask him about Chappaquiddick. But I did ask Dizzy Gillespie about the problems of ecology. His answers meant more to the young people who watch my show than anything a forest ranger or naturalist could say. Their attitude is, "That's what their job is. They're paid to say that. Let's hear from somebody who's willing to tackle the issues on his own hook." I didn't think The Womens' Liberation officials did their cause much good on my show. They limited it, made it seem private, and almost petty. But when a young social worker talked about the difficulty qualified women like her have in getting a decent job, people took notice.

**Harmony is not a matter of avoiding issues, nor is it a matter of delaying decisions.** The worst thing you can do to someone who asks your help is to put him off in a limbo of some kind. Some people won't take a hint, so you have to be firm. And you have to know your reasons. I don't rely on my own judgment when people think I have that much power over their lives. I consult my brain trust.

But I never say I don't know if someone wants my decision. I'm never unsure about that. Because I act swiftly on a request I clear the air for them to go on to the next step. If worse comes to worst, and you can't find the information you need, and you can't face another request and another ringing phone, take the advice that George Miller used to give young copywriters who were trying to come up with scintillating adjectives for the newest brand of soap: Go out to a movie. When life is just too much, and crises are piling on top of crises, I sneak out to a Forty-second Street movie house. Not to the porno palaces which abound around here, but to a cowboy or adventure flick. And you know something? When I get back to the office I find that nothing has stopped without me. Life goes on. It's positively eerie.

**You've got to have harmony in your own life to find it in others.** Spend time with people you can relax with. Don't mix with those who are always trying to con you, who make you keep your defenses up. Leslie Gourse writes about one of my old buddies, "Hal's soles used to be hanging off, his shirt came through a torn seam in his jacket, and he never wore a tie. 'Want to borrow a tie?' Joe once asked him with a mischievous smile, as he was taking him out for a steak dinner in a dark restaurant. 'My kind of people,' Joe says." Can you stand this old favorite of mine? It makes sense.

*Friends*

'Twould never do for God to live across the street
Or in the house next door, where we should daily
  meet;
So in his wisdom and in his love he sometimes sends
His angels kind to walk with us—we call them friends.

When trouble comes, or loss, when grief is ours to bear,
They come, our friends, with words of cheer our load
  to share.

How could we face defeat without a friend's caress?
Had we no friend to praise, how bare would be
success.

'Tis not God's plan that we shall see him face to face;
Yet he would hedge us in his abounding grace,
And so his messengers of love to earth he sends—
They're angels, but we know it not and call them
"friends."

Remember that line: Had we no friends to praise how bare would be success. Make no "threats of hostile confrontation," as John J. O'Connor sums up our atmosphere on the show, and you'll have friends to share your smallest success. Give praise away freely—it's too hot to handle.

# Sixteen
*
# Wing It

I have a divided mind about preambles. I have a feeling, on the one hand, that an excessive buildup steals the thunder of what it's building up to; and, on the other hand, that preparation is everything. It may not look that way, but I do prepare my shows thoroughly. I happen to prefer the backs of unopened mail to a clipboard, but the result is the same. I have a sketch of where I'm going, what my guests have in mind, what subjects should be raised. Still I say, "Wing it!" And there's no contradiction; let's have a preamble, I say, but let's take off from there into unexplored territory.

Helen Hayes once told me how she prepared so thoroughly for each role that she had to remind herself every now and then who she really was. But the theater is different from a conversation, unless it's ad-lib theater. And still the similarities remain: Once you've immersed yourself in your role—whatever the role, however loose—then you're unfettered by a script. You wing it.

The best moments on my show just grew out of situations. No gags were set up. No fixed opinions were rehearsed. No lines were memorized. No script was followed. Here are my Golden Dozen guests from twenty-five years of TVing, with some of the things they've said.

Jack Kennedy: Don't ever ask an Irishman how old he is, he's liable to tell you the truth.

Maurice Chevalier: Thank heaven for older girls, too.

Eddie Cantor: It's a big country—too big for people with little hearts and little ideas.

Judy Garland: I never grew up, thank God. I'm a kid, they say, yeah, I am. I am.

Louis Armstrong: (humming) I tell those cats, yeah you *can* take that away from me. You can, you can. (Speaking of the IRS).

Elizabeth Taylor: Mike Todd was the most American man ever made, and he was made in America. An American he-man, I kid you not.

Bing Crosby: (off-camera) Yeah, let's wing it—that's what I've been doin' all my life.

Joe Louis: I was never angry in the ring—I don't know what they mean by the "killer instinct"—only my fists are mean.

Barbra Streisand: Eat your heart out, Liz Taylor. Here I come.

Shirley Temple: If I get their attention because I'm Shirley Temple, that's all right. It's what I do after that, that I care about

Jack Benny: New York is where I belong—we're in New York, aren't we?

Cary Grant: I watch the old movies, as long as I'm not in 'em. . . . That's why I like really *old* ones—then I'm never surprised by showing up accidentally.

That's my Golden Group. I'd like to make it a baker's dozen, plus one, if I could only get these two: Jimmy Cagney and Greta Garbo. Cagney and my father went to P.S. 158 together, if that means anything. But Jimmy's a busy man nowadays—he has no reason to leave his beautiful home for Forty-second Street. Greta, I'm still hoping. . . . When we meet in the street, we say hello. It ends there.

I find it particularly interesting that the old cowboys were "wingers" on the show. I guess they were used to the naturalness of the old B films. Gene Autry, Tex Ritter, Tim McCoy, Bill Boyd, Roy Rogers, and others I've mentioned already could talk off the cuff quite readily. And they could talk as cowboys, because that's what they really were.

Dong Kingman always impressed me with the ease of his conversation, in fact, seeming, as simple as his art. That's the thing about winging it—it looks so simple you think anybody can do it. But it comes from a well-rehearsed mind, not a well-rehearsed tongue. Dong told me how he disposed of a stubborn salesman once, in a way that would have seemed outrageous to anyone but the playful Mr. Kingman. A public relations man had been hounding him for weeks, promising all sorts of publicity if Dong would only sign on the dotted line. Having all the publicity he needed, but not wishing to say no outright, Dong offered to play the man a game of chess, on the condition that if he lost he would sign and if he won he would be spared further calls. To make it a matter of record, the game was played in the foyer of Jack and Charley's "21" Club—where Mr. Kingman had the pleasure of publicly dispatching his adversary. That's also "winging it."

There's an aura of winging it in those unsightly, but intriguing, hand-made homes that young people build on the backs of pickup trucks and vans. Bubble windows pop out here and there; log cabins on wheels loom up ahead of you at traffic lights. I must be somewhat conventional in my thinking, because I can't imagine that these do-it-yourself contraptions look good even to their owners. Nevertheless, I salute the spirit behind them and only hope a log doesn't fly off as they roll down the parkway.

You can see what I'm building up to. Conventional though I may seem, I admire and encourage the unconventional in others. I welcome spontaneity, verve, dash, flavor; but the keynote is naturalness.

A lesson in naturalness is to be learned in the way the hit songs were mostly "flip sides" of the songs that were supposed to make it. "Rudolph the Red-Nosed Reindeer" was a flip side, an afterthought. It's an education to go through the old 78s and try to guess which side the hit song was supposed to be. The lesson seems clear enough: When the performers were relaxed and unfettered, they were able to sing with inspiration. Or is the public taste just so fickle that a composer or musician or producer never really knows what will take the public's fancy? I'll bet that someone who knows what naturalness is knows what the public will want.

The public reacts on its guts. Guts may mean a catchy tune, a heart-grabbing story, an upbeat ending. **But all the great performers know what the public wants—because at bottom it's what** they **want.** They know when they've got something going. They know when they've struck a false note. They know when they've tried to float one past the audience. They know, because they're not very different from their audience.

So it's no mystery that I have the audience I have. Somebody once said the intellectuals disdain me. Well, I disdain them right back. I should correct that statement slightly. I disdain the *self-proclaimed* intellectuals right back.

I am Joe Franklin. My name is common, and so am I. I marvel that I have been able to make a living at the thing I wanted to do from my childhood. I am surprised by each new day, counting the years I have been in this supposedly cutthroat business. I am astounded by the positive commentary I get, from the best papers and reviewers. I am rewarded day in and day out by people who say I have helped them. I am rewarded by, yes, by the advertisers on the program—not only by their continuing orders, their contracts, but by the response I get when I visit their stores and meet long lines of their customers.

Among my advertisers is the Martin Paint Stores, Inc. I've always said that paint is like doughnuts—you buy it where you can get it most conveniently. But this paint happens to be better, not just more convenient So I stick out my neck for them. Jerry Shier, executive vice president of Martin Paint Stores, was the first "merchant" to do his own television commercials Today thousands are following this innovation—which, I must confess, we created.

Another advertiser might be a newcomer who can't see beyond one thirty-second spot. That's the man I want to nudge along. I'm a sucker for him, maybe because I've been there. But I don't think my big advertisers resent my personal feeling for the little guy. Now, they let *me* wing it. Which is to say that they're winging it, not playing it by the numbers.

I'll tell you all about the uneventful parts of my life, too, if you ask me. It's what my life has touched that's more interesting. Did you ever hear of Earl Cooley? Not likely, but he's the guy who invented the book clubs. When he wanted to give a good send-off to a book, he'd call. Then he took a wife who was worth going to California for. He'd call me even from there. Then he stopped calling. He was ill and his bride was concerned. Then she called to tell me his life was over. I've had a funny sad feeling about book clubs ever since.

And I miss jazz! And I miss cowboy movies! And I miss Block and Smith and Whiteman! My mentors! Don't think you'll ever miss someone the way I miss them. That's no show-biz pride. And I miss children. I know all too well what kids meant to radio and early TV. I remember Huddie Ledbetter—Leadbelly—playing and singing for the kids down in the Village all weekend and all night, if need be. The Midnight Special is gonna shine its light on you. Its ever lovin' light.

Sometimes you need to prod yourself in some little way if you're going to keep up on that high plane of action. I take my shoes off before I slip into my panel seat on the show. A superstition, I guess. But I've discovered this about times that could be tense or difficult: **Little rituals are important in helping you feel relaxed and natural.** It's something like the batters who tap the plate or rub out part of the batter's box. When I can't seem to get started on an idea for a show or a talk or a column I go back down my own memory lane. The psychologists call it free association. The advertising agencies call it brainstorming. You start somewhere, anywhere, and let one idea lead to another. The important part is to never reject an idea out of hand. Let it develop. Don't dismiss what someone suggests just because you think you've heard it all before. He may be going somewhere else with it. Use any device that comes to mind to keep the ball rolling. It may be a book, an old record, a tennis racket, a sweater. Take a walk around the block. Rearrange the furniture. Dust that picture on the wall. Do the things that have worked before.

I like to collect favorite quotations (in addition to all those other collections of mine). I don't mean great pieces of rhetoric, but funny things, odd descriptions, little jokes, puns, limericks, bon mots, and bloopers. This kind of word-play especially tickles me:

*How to Handle a Woman Electrically*

If she wants to be an angel—Transformer.
If she'll meet you halfway—Receiver.
If she hits the ceiling—Condenser.
If she has to get out of the house—Discharger.
When she's in error—Rectifier.
When she wants to have a baby—Generator.

I find such light, innocuous material, even cornball lines like these, can stir up good ideas. And the more you can remember the better. I can never thank the teacher enough who made me memorize a few lines of Shakespeare in school. They come to my mind at the oddest moments, and then I'm curious to find out again what the rest of the poem or play is about. So I dust off the old books in search of the source. The more you have floating around in your head, the easier it is to wing it—to leap from one odd bit of information to another.

I secretly envy those serious students of Shakespeare who can reel off line after line, then quote the play, the act, and the verse. Here's a favorite of mine I have to look up for the exact words, but I'll bet it means more to me than you'd ever guess:

> Once more unto the breach, dear friends, once more,
> Or close the wall up with our English dead.
> In peace there's nothing so becomes a man
> As modest stillness and humility;
> But when the blast of war blows in our ears,
> Then imitate the action of the tiger;
> Stiffen the sinews, summon up the blood,
> Disguise fair nature with hard-favour'd rage; . . .

For the record, this is the beginning of Act III, Scene I, of *Henry V.* It expresses more than the call to action of the warrior: It's the call to action of any job. To me it says match your demeanor to your task. When you're called to arms, "imitate the action of the tiger." If you're a salesman, sell for all you're worth. If you're a disc jockey, spin 'em the way you like 'em. And if you're Joe Franklin, preside over your show with "modest stillness and humility."

It's difficult to say things off the cuff in print. There's

so much permanence, so much power, in the printed word, even in a newspaper. Tell your best friend a personal secret twenty times, and when it's printed in the local shopping news he'll begin to take it seriously.

So, though I've been trying to talk off the cuff here, I confess I can't do in print what I can on a talk show. I've rehearsed this chapter. I've plotted what I was going to say. I've searched my memory for pieces of advice to pass on to you. I've looked up quotations. Yet I find I'm coming to a conclusion that I didn't forsee at the start. The reason I like to ad lib and to fly by the seat of my pants is that personal combat is my game. That's also why it's difficult to get the point across in print. I like to deal person to person. The combat may not be physical, and certainly isn't in anger; yet even in my most harmonious moments it's always there. It's the gentle combat of drawing out someone's inner feelings. In Robert Louis Stevenson's words—

> The spice of life is battle; the friendliest relations are still a kind of contest; and if we would not forgo all that is valuable in our lot, we must continually face some other person, eye to eye, and wrestle a fall whether in love or enmity. It is still by force of body, or power of character or intellect, that we attain to worthy pleasures. Men and women contend for each other in the lists of love, like rival mesmerists; the active and adroit decide their challenges in the sports of the body; and the sedentary sit down to chess or conversation.

How about a friendly conversation?

# Seventeen

*

# Remember Where You Came From

Remember. Recall your beginnings. Relive your past. Revel in your upbringing. Return to the simple things. Rerun your life in slow motion, without interruption by commercials for yourself, without retractions. Fill yourself up with remembering.

Do you remember taking naps in a dark room, wondering why the big people had this great thing about little people lying down in the middle of the day? Do you remember feeling better because of it, or do you remember faking the sleep, the eyes closed, the breath steady? Did you hear the elders talking secret talks you weren't supposed to hear? Now, do you remember any of it?

Remember pain, the first sting of a burnt finger on

the wood-burning stove, the split thumbnail you got trying to catch a baseball, the itch of poison ivy or poison oak, the unjust spanking. Remember the release of pain, the ice cream after your tonsillectomy, the love of relatives you never knew, the jars of hard candy, the little wax bottles of sweet liquid. Recall the approval of adults.

Listen to your memories. Dwell on childhood experiences. Think of your fears in the middle of the night. Remember the shock of institutions, the schoolyard, the knowledgeability of older brothers and sisters, the recess that nobody announced, the return bell that nobody told you about. Remember the big kids and their manner. Remember everything that took you away from your mother and father and your home and your room and your daily bread. Remember that you were once free in their grace and their succor.

Remember people before you, for all people are before you in one way or another. Remember Emily Dickinson and Emily Post. Remember not to be facetious when you should be serious. But enjoy it anyway.

**Remember, because you will repeat your past.** Think of life as a ring that always comes back to the beginning. Ring around the rosey. Ashes, ashes, all fall down. Remember man that thou art dust. Remember that in the ring of life nothing is washed out. Remember without becoming sacrosanct.

Always place present happiness against past pleasures. Do not downgrade the present because the past has lost its thorns. Remember for the future. Remember for your grandchildren. Remember all the little friends you knew whom you will never see again: You will never repeat that first expression of love for them.

Think of Christmases if you have ever prepared a Christmas, or a celebration of any kind. Think of your astonishment at the presentation of gifts. Think of your anticipation, remember your concern. Go back to the very beginning of your memory. Try to recall that very first glow of recognition of some thought. It must have been some change: a moving of the household, a visit by a relative, a stern word when none was called for. When you see your grandchildren doing what you did, see yourself in a new light. See what may be *their* first glow of recognition. If you can't remember anything else, recall any Christmas.

Repeat what you do well. Don't be ashamed of going over the well-worn routines of your day. Lying in bed sleepless, recount the accomplishments of your day, however trivial they may seem. Think of that pleasant conversation you had at lunch, or even that single bon mot. At the very least such thoughts tend to help you sleep, and to sweeten your dreams. And to confirm you in a direction that apparently works for you.

**Remember, because you are a bearer of good news for future generations.** The important information never seems to find its way into books. Man was once only an oral historian. Before printing presses or even paper were invented, he passed along his literature by word of mouth. I believe that he still passes down the real truth by word of mouth. From father to daughter, from mother to son, from uncle to nephew, from grandmother to grandson the story of life is planted in the bed of humanity's memory. Individual events and dates and names of generals are best left to books.

Of course, the story of life we hear from those who care about us, stories of their own experiences are often colored by their wishes and fears. William James puts it clearly—

> The most frequent source of false memory is the accounts we give to others of our experiences. Such acts we almost always make more simple and more interesting than the truth. We quote what we should have said or done rather than what we really said or did; and in the first telling we may be fully aware of the distinction, but ere long the fiction expels the reality from memory and reigns in its stead alone. We think of what we wish had happened, of possible interpretations of acts, and soon we are unable to distinguish between things that actually happened and our own thoughts about what might have occurred.

But knowing all this, don't be discouraged about the important things in your memory; they are the values and impressions that are formed in you like the shape of a vase turning on a spindle.

When you remember where you came from, your mind goes back not simply to your family home or to your grandmother's stories, but to her grandmother. And one day, some three or four generations hence, what you are doing now will be working in the memory of perhaps hundreds of offspring. Think of it: a span of several hundred years of people, linked by the thread of memory.

Though not critical to that river of values that flows in us, genealogies are fun, and they and any other kinds of printed records are useful in helping you remember those values. Use photographs. In the lines of your grandfather's face you will see more than in the writings of any historian. Use the museums, the art galleries, the curio shops. All these are efforts at recreating memory. Have you gone back to your own baby book, if you were lucky enough to have one? How silly, that locket of hair from your first haircut, that printed announcement of your birth! But also how charged with the sentiments and values of those who put them there.

I know that scrapbooks and baby books and other mementos aren't supposed to be manly. Men are supposed to remember baseball players and boxers. They should also be able to call to mind great Presidents, inventors, writers. But why do we spend so much time remembering where we *didn't* come from? We might have seen Babe Ruth, with two strikes on him, pointing his bat to right centerfield just before stroking that famous home run, but that isn't where *we* came from. Most of us came from schoolyards or sandlots where dramatic home runs never happened. So I'm not saying please remember just anything about the past. Remember your *personal* past. Remember writers who touched you, and how they touched you—not how they touched the critics.

Resist the destruction of the landmarks that physically touched your past, and preserve them for the children of your children. Don't give in to change for the sake of change. Isn't a good part of our society like a self-indulgent child? We devour delicious-looking chocolates of progress. We stuff ourselves with the candy of commercialism. We throw up glass and chrome boxes fifty stories high because there is a market for the offices they contain—they are delicious to someone. But most of us have to face the outside of those boxes as our landscape without anyone having consulted us on the matter. Hold on to the Grand Central Stations of our world until it is shown that we can leave something better to our progeny.

**Remember where you came from, because it is the well of your inspiration.** The famous eventually give us an account of their lives; thank them for it. I'm sure that in most cases they are motivated by the desire to share their good fortune. The ninety-nine and forty-four one hundredths percent who never write their memoirs can still pass them down to their friends and family. They can tell their old stories over and over. They can recount the same emotion-laden turning points of their growing up. Their eyes well with tears, their throats choke at the flicker of those memories. And we let them, because we are then fused with their lives and we will someday be able to incorporate their being into our own small creations, our gifts to others.

You know those cards that are passed around offices when someone is leaving? Everyone puts his name on them somewhere, and maybe even a cute remark. Think of how many people have put their imprint on you, on your person, if you have only passed your "card" around freely. What a wonderful thing it is to know that everything you are now engaged in is making its mark on you. Your dullest task is one small stone in your wall of recollections. Take it out from the wall, and even the largest boulders will be weaker. But polish it and set it carefully in place, and one day you can count on its proving itself a meaningful experience.

What unusual things come from autobiographies! What a different view we receive of someone when he writes about an event thirty or forty years later. We find that when we were thinking him a hero, he wasn't all that sure of himself. We discover how inspiration comes from within: from memories of your youth, and your inexplicable behavior in growing up, from your struggles to come to terms with a world you did not create, or a transition from singleness to married life or vice-versa. **Inspiration isn't the domain of only writers and artists.** It exists in the notebooks and diaries, letters and postcards of ordinary people, too. Have you forgotten the love notes you once wrote in school? Have you tossed into the wastebasket of oblivion the scribbles on textbook covers and the doodles on the backs of assignment sheets?

Mark Twain wrote an autobiography of great warmth, not the least part of which was the inclusion of a biography of him by his fourteen-year-old daughter, Susy. He was writing this part of his autobiography in 1906, some twenty years after Susy's childhood account of him, ten years after her death.

> She did this work in her bedroom at night, and kept her record hidden. After a little, the mother discovered it and filched it, and let me see it; then told Susy what she had done, and how pleased I was and how proud. I remember that time with a deep pleasure. I had had compliments before, but none that touched me like this;

> none that could approach it for value in my eyes. It has kept that place always since. I have no compliment, no praise, no tribute from any source, that was so precious to me as this one, and still is. As I read it now, after all these many years, it is still a king's message to me, and brings me the same dear surprise it brought me then—with the pathos added of the thought that the eager and hasty hand that sketched it and scrawled it will not touch mine again—and I feel as the humble and unexpectant must feel when their eyes fall upon the edict that raises them to the ranks of the noble.
>
> Yesterday while I was rummaging in a pile of ancient note-books of mine which I had not seen for years, I came across a reference to that biography. It is quite evident that several times, at breakfast and dinner, in those long-past days, I was posing for the biography. In fact, I clearly remember that I *was* doing that—and I also remember that Susy detected it. I remember saying a very smart thing, with a good deal of an air, at the breakfast table one morning, and that Susy observed to her mother privately, a little later, that papa was doing that for the biography.

What a great reason for resurrecting the institution of having breakfast together as a family. Can't you just picture the fourteen-year-old saying later, "Papa was doing that for the biography"? It wouldn't be fair not to include some of Susy's observations:

> We are a very happy family. We consist of Papa, Mamma, Jean, Clara, and me. It is Papa I am writing about, and I shall have no trouble in not knowing what to say about him, as he is a very striking character. . . . Papa's favorite game is billiards, and when he is tired and wishes to rest himself he stays up all night and

plays billiards, it seems to rest his head. He smokes a great deal almost incessantly. He has the mind of an author exactly, some of the simplest things he can't understand. Our burglar alarm is often out of order, and Papa has been obliged to take the mahogany room off from the alarm altogether for a time, because the burglar alarm has been in the habit of ringing even when the mahogany-room window was closed. At length he thought that perhaps the burglar alarm might be in order, and he decided to try and see; accordingly he put it on and then went down and opened the window; consequently the alarm bell rang, it would even if the alarm had been in order. Papa went despairingly upstairs and said to mamma, "Livy, the mahogany room won't go on. I have just opened the window to see." "Why, Youth," mamma replied. "If you've opened the window, why of course the alarm will ring!"

"That's why I've opened it for, why I just went down to see if it would ring!"

Mamma tried to explain to Papa that when he wanted to go and see whether the alarm would ring while the window was closed he *mustn't* go and open the window—but in vain, Papa couldn't understand. . . .

Well, that's a part of where we all came from, from people like Mark Twain and Susy Clemens. And that is what prompts me to say, finally—

**Remember, because it will stabilize you.** Remember that every age has its malcontents of various stripes, for whom nothing is up to standard. There are always those who mock the common man for his vulgarity, for his maudlin responses and unfashionableness. They see workers in their baggy suit coats, shoveling gravel along back-country Irish roads, and smile condescendingly. They are bored with baseball, or they find it a parable, but they will never know the feeling of giving up part of themselves to a team. They are chatty, but don't talk; they disdain the common entertainments. Children are an intrusion in their pursuits. They are looking for a whole new society of some sort without for a minute supposing that this one, even with improvements, is worth continuing. Unfortunately, "they" are you, and me. Aren't they? Some of the time? Remembering where we came from helps bring us down from the clouds, helps us see that what pleased us long ago, and our friends from history before us, will please us again, and is more basic and more within reach of ordinary souls.

How long does it take to forget a burnt-out love? To recover from rejection? From loneliness? From the dull pain in the pit of the stomach when someone's voice suddenly turns cold and rational and final? We all know that all such pain will soften in time; what we need reminding about is that we can speed up time and its healing by—more remembrance! Remember where you came from without fear of remorse or shame. Remember embarrassments and dishonor! Dwell on defeat, don't just nibble at it, because it's easily consumed. This is the power of memory: to devour the unconscious resentment of the past, to prepare a welcome for the arrival of the future.

# Eighteen
*

# Happiness Avenue

Happiness Avenue is just around the corner, folks. See that tall building on the left, with people running madly in and out? That's the famous Money Building. And that big park that stretches out on our right as far as the eye can see is Experience Land. It takes years to get through; one day at a time is all they'll let you travel. Watch out for the traffic on the Street of Dreams! It's really busy today. What'd you say? When will we get to Happiness Avenue? Well, you see, it's a funny street. Somebody keeps tearing it up to put in new sewers or something. And just about when you think you're on it, a barricade goes up for some kind of parade. But, like I say, it's just around the corner. I've been doing this tour nearly all my life and I know I'll get to see it someday.

Happiness is just a thing called Joe, the song says, but don't you believe it. Back in school somewhere I learned that happiness isn't anything. It's the nice feeling along the way, but not a goal or the result of any particular combination of events. The Philosopher (I capitalize his name the way the medieval writers did who were assured there was only one—Mr. Aristotle) said that happiness comes by not seeking it. Our founding fathers got it wrong—we can't talk of the pursuit of happiness but the happiness of pursuit.

Of course, it's easy to use the word in its narrow meaning. When a guy sells his house because he wants to move to a quiet place in the country, and another guy buys it to be nearer his work, and the price is right, the real-estate people pronounce the deal a success by saying, "Both parties are happy." They're really only happy about the deal. And I'm always happy when I wake up in the morning, even though I may be going through what people commonly call an unhappy period in my life. But let's talk about that broad state of general happiness that is so elusive.

**I don't think sad is the opposite of happy.** We don't come into this world neutral. The dice are loaded for human beings: they're by nature *doers*. To be alive means to be looking for something, experiencing something, moving ahead, moving back, improving, dissipating. Happiness is the feeling that comes when what we're doing is what is right for us, whatever fits our definition. A bumper sticker reads, "I am my definition of myself." The opposite of happiness is the feeling of awkwardness, of being out of kilter. But you can be sad, in the normal sense of the word, and at the same time be in focus with what you are and hence be happy in the best sense of the word.

I used to know an old Irishman, the father of a schoolmate of mine, who didn't feel right unless he was melancholy. If things were going too well and there was no trouble on the horizon, he felt out of sorts. Time was heavy on his hands. He would fidget and try to make up some kind of trouble. Will Rogers, speaking of another fellow, described him perfectly—

> John would go down to the main street bank in the morning to consult with the men in the vested suits, and it always made him feel better. They'd tell him how the market was down and he'd have to bring some more green paper in to replace the big fancy white paper his mining shares were printed on, and it'd give John something to do and fuss about. Fussin' was good for him. If he didn't have the banks to fuss about he'd probably make a fool of himself at the saloon or playin' poker for a handful of pennies.

There's a whole gamut of emotions people usually lump together into what they call sadness. But I know that I'm often hurt or distressed or annoyed or disgusted but none of those feelings detracts from my happiness. It's just part of my "definition of myself" to experience all those emotions. **You might say having a truly sad moment also makes me happy.**

The movies are constantly trying to define happiness for us. A happy ending is often tacked on to a tragic script to help the box office—because people *want* to see people achieve what's inside them. They sense the ultimate unhappiness—when two people "meant for each other" are cruelly separated by fate.

Often the directors or front-office people who tamper with an unhappy ending are closer to life than the writers. (Heresy! I'll hear about this!) The Academy Award winning *Casablanca* was written with two different endings, supposedly so that Ingrid Bergman would be in doubt up to the very end. It's worth exploring the tensions of this famous ending, which had to deal with the various degrees of happiness of four very diverse people.

Humphrey Bogart and Ingrid Bergman are accidentally thrown together in North Africa, a year and a half after their brief idyll in Paris. There is bitterness between them; we learn that Bogart was stood up by Bergman as they planned to leave Paris before the German occupation. A song ("*their* song") symbolizes their heartbreak, as sung and played by Dooley Wilson, Bogart's cabaret performer:

> BERGMAN: *(whispering)* Play it, Sam. Play "As Time Goes By.". . .
>
> WILSON: Oh I can't remember it, Miss Elsa. I'm a little rusty on it.
>
> BERGMAN: I'll hum it for you. *(hums)*
>
> WILSON: "It's still the same old story . . ." *(sings song to completion.)*

The background of the movie's plot unfolds as a flashback in the middle of the dramatic confrontation of the two ex-lovers. The world-weary Bogart is shaken by Bergman's sudden appearance in his night club, although he suspects something is brewing from having overheard Wilson tinkering around with "As Time Goes By." His bitterness erupts. Bergman's loyalty ebbs back and forth as everyone is swept into Rick's Place for a bit of gambling and sloshing, and as underground hero Paul Henried, Bergman's reason for remaining in Paris, toasts the French Resistance. Would Bogart and Bergman escape together after all? Would Henreid see a higher call to duty, or would he be unable to go on without Bergman at his side? Would the cynical Claude Rains capture any or all of them, or would he turn patriot in the end?

The answer was hidden in the fog-shrouded Casablanca airport. The script was so carefully done that a number of endings could have been expected from the preceding action. But happiness, I firmly believe, triumphed. Bogart and Rains walked off arm in arm in a symbiotic cynicism. Bergman's mind was made up for her by Bogart's last act of unselfishness. And I think she was needed to bolster the quixotic Mr. Henreid, whose nobility had begun to sag. At least that's my reading of things, and I'm still suspended by the unresolved love affair of Bogart and Bergman.

Thank God they didn't decide to make a sequel, you know, Henreid a martyr in the liberation of Paris, Bogart rolling in on a tank, Bergman searching wildly through the crowds on the Champs Élysées, a bear-hug reunion, and, spare us O Lord, a champagne bridal-suite toast with the epithalamium, rendered by Dooley, drifting through the French doors from a corner bistro: "The fundamental things apply . . ."

I prefer to remain in suspense, to have the sequel left to my imagination. I like a little melancholy. I am thankful for honest sadness in life, even my own. I am thankful for honest criticism.

Every time someone does a magazine or newspaper profile of me, I love the publicity but I cringe at what a promotion it is for me. After all, I work for my station and their advertisers, not for myself. A lot of TV hosts don't last because they're only interested in feathering their nests. They put all their friends on the show and start parading a little clique of admirers in front of the camera. The attitude they think is so well concealed comes shining through. You really *can't* conceal any attitude for very long. And that applies to all of life, not just to television. Abe Lincoln said it, I think: God gave you your nose but you make your own face.

The article about me in *The New Yorker*, a beautifully written piece, bothered me at first. Boy, was I flattered to be thought worthy of a profile! But am I really the zany character that comes through in parts like this?

> On the air, Joe has effusive praise for everything and everybody, and is as mild and friendly as a cocker spaniel. In his office, he is still friendly, but there is an edge of impatience in all his transactions and an air of authority in his voice. He keeps most of his phone calls short, and his goodbyes tend to be barked commands. He always slams the phone into its cradle, with a sudden pouncing movement, as though he were swatting flies with the receiver. The hubbub in the office is punctuated all day by the sound of Joe's explosive goodbyes: "Don't forget!" *Bang!* "Wait for my call!" *Bang!* "Keep me in touch!" *Bang!* "God bless you!" *Bang!*

The day after I read that I began dropping the receiver down like a chess player removing his king from an ambush instead of gobbling up a loose queen.

I've had my share of unfriendly criticism, too. I'll give you three good examples.

Joan Rivers had been on my show perhaps forty times before she had the opportunity to size me up in print. Bear in mind that part of her avowed reason for coming on the show was to study my techniques in preparation for launching her own talk show. She wrote something like this: "I like to watch Joe Franklin for the same reason I like to watch Julia Child drop a lamb chop. I think if Franklin had Brazil '66 on his show, he'd ask them where they came from," implying in her sarcasm that I would actually pose such a question. I've never had Brazil '66 on, but, as a matter of fact, it wouldn't be a bad question to ask the group, since there's a popular misconception that they're all Brazilian. Two things I'm sure of: (1) they come from different parts of the world, and (2) Joan Rivers won't be invited to my show anymore.

Only twice in my life did I ever consider suing for something said about me in print. First there was Al Morgan, just back from a national tour to plug his book. In an article in *TV Guide* comparing TV interviewers he'd had during that experience, he misquoted me eight times in statements I'd made during his appearance on my show. I ignored it, but my station wanted to set the record straight. When they reviewed the tapes, they suggested I take legal action—against the author, not *TV Guide.* So I did. Mr. Morgan's apology promptly appeared in the magazine, and what I won from the lawsuit I donated to charity.

Then there was George Frazier, who gave me a scurrilous roasting in his newspaper column. I attributed it to professional jealousy, since, as I was later informed, he had wanted to emcee the Newport Jazz Festival, which impressario George Wein had invited me to handle. I thought about it for a long time, and then I discovered that an executive at the paper was prepared to dismiss Frazier if one more lawsuit were brought against him. So I buried my pride and forgot the whole matter. I never regretted that decision, because within a year the man was dead. To this day I am mystified and hurt that two people, to whom both privately and during their appearances on my program I demonstrated admiration and respect, would turn on me with such venom.

Something else that disheartens me is, when an obvious attraction comes to town—the star of a new motion picture or the author of a best-seller—to have my show ignored. Rod Steiger went on practically every talk show on the Eastern Seaboard for his movie *W. C. Fields and Me,* a subject close to my heart, but his bookers at the film company chose not to submit him to me. Not only could I probably have sold 40,000 or 50,000 tickets for them that they couldn't have sold any other way, but I also felt I had let my audience down, since this is the kind of thing I promise to bring them.

Peter Bogdanovich looked down his nose at us after he had risen from being a writer of program notes for me to becoming a Hollywood director. His lady, Cybil Sheppard, had been on my show many times as a model and young actress, and was scheduled to appear again to promote the film *At Long Last Love,* in which she was co-starring. An embarrassed publicity agent of hers called at the last minute to beg off—for reasons of health. But he whispered the real reason to me—Mr. Bogdanovich had crossed my show off her list, deeming my "plug" not too necessary. Would it be unkind to add that both films were financial disasters?

But things do work out for the best in the long run. I sent Pop out for hamburgers the other day, for a young lady who wanted all the trimmings. In the hubbub of ringing phones, the message got garbled, and Pop came back with juicy burgers—plain. What could I say? I apologized and said, "Pop, you're right. We're better off without onions."

"How's that, Joe?" she laughed.

"Sweetheart, how would those onions go over on that big date tonight?"

"What big date?"

"There are two tickets waiting for you at the Majestic, and a mysterious young man who's never met you but is big, verrry big in Hollywood. You want to try it blind?" I hadn't thought of it before the onions came up, but there *was* a gentleman without escort in town for a few days and he *did* make the date when I called him a few minutes later. I can be more specific about other happy endings.

Back in 1963, Lainie Kazan was moping around my office on the verge of what I thought would be a sensational career. She was a stand-in for you know who in *Funny Girl*, but all she did was stand and wait. In one of her darker moods I predicted she would get her chance and would be a hit. And she didn't give up. Within two weeks she got a last-minute call. I remember standing at the back of the theater when the change in actresses was announced. The crowd hissed and booed. They wanted to see the star. They'd paid their money to be able to tell the neighbors the next morning that they'd seen the biggest star on Broadway. A few left. "Don't quit now," I said to myself, as if somehow I was in debt to her for my encouragement. It was a solid performance. When the final curtain came down, the audience roared. She was on her way.

Happiness seems to consist in being excited about what you've got going for you, taking pleasure in others' happiness as well, and not confusing the two. In this competitive business, it's hard not to feel that everybody else's success is achieved at your expense. If every actress turns out to be a sensation, how can you get your nose in the tent? The answer is that talent breeds talent. That's why there are such things as Golden Ages, when happiness is never achieved at the expense of someone else, but flourishes among happy people.

# Nineteen

*

# June and January

Jazz and the art of the fugue have at least one thing in common—they are often appreciated by the same people. The reason they're not more universally accepted, I think, is largely accidental; with enough exposure to any art form, almost anyone can take pleasure in it. All this is to introduce my theory about what makes for a good conversation. I believe in the clash of opposites, June and January, rather than getting people together who "have similar interests."

Leopold Stokowski was one of my most thrilling guests, a man of universal interests and complete self-assurance. We talked about the swing era and progressive jazz and rock and roll. Some would say I didn't know enough about symphonic music to discuss it.

The real reason, in fact, was that I had a young jazz pianist on that show, and I knew Mr. Stokowski preferred to talk about what interested other people as well as himself.

There is nothing more depressing than watching someone become fixed in a pattern, and I find the usual reason for the fixing is a person's becoming preoccupied with a limited field of interest. Uncle Don, star of an early radio program for kids, used to say things like this to his audience (and their parents):

> Never teast and pout all day,
> Suppose your face should freeze that way.

Faces are freezing all over town, hearts are freezing, minds are freezing, because people are so intent on their own interests they can't listen to what anyone else has to say.

(Uncle Don himself was the victim of the kind of narrowmindedness that leads to injustice. In the early days of radio, audiences were fascinated by what went on when the mike was off. Bloopers were the talk of cocktail parties everywhere. Someone fabricated a story that, at the end of a broadcast, Uncle Don, thinking the mike was off, had said, "There! I guess that'll hold the little bastards!" A prominent wire service picked up the story and it spread like lightning. Uncle Don was branded a fraud; his career dwindled and he died of a broken heart. It didn't matter to those who had invented the story that it might be a bad joke with a lot of grave consequences. They were interested in the joke, not in Uncle Don.)

The early movie studios were certainly tolerant of any and all interests a person might have. They were polyglot assemblages of vaudevillians, Shakespearean actors, jugglers (W. C. Fields and Buster Keaton, no less!), bareback-horse riders, dancers, corporation lawyers, and medicine men, to mention only a few. They spoke different languages but sharpened their talents accordingly. Gene Fowler tells about the early stars of Sennett's studio, who swam together now and again in the pool just off their dressing rooms. There were Marie Dressler, Charles Chaplin, Wallace Beery, Gloria Swanson, Fatty Arbuckle, Mabel Normand, Ford Sterling, Harry Langdon, Phyllis Haver, and Eddie Foy and family. There were W. C. Fields, Ben Turpin, Mack Swain, Chester Conklin, Joe Jackson, Al St. John, and Harold Lloyd. Had enough? There were also Willie Collier, Sr., Sam Bernard, Hale Hamilton, Raymond Hitchcock, Fred Mace, Weber and Fields, Lew Cody, Marie Prevost, Louise Fazenda, Syd Chaplin, Bobby Dunn, Polly Moran, Bebe Daniels, Eddie Quillan, Buster Keaton, Charlie Murray, and Hal Roach. Fowler follows this dazzling array of talent with a description of how the pool looked a mere ten years after the heyday of the Sennett studio:

> One peers over the crumbling ledge to see an obscene medley of warped, rusty gutters, sere palm leaves, tin cans, a bucket with remnants of ancient mortar bulging its bottom, discarded wash tubs, a section of bashed-in stove pipe, the dented hood of an automobile radiator of a forgotten make, the rim of a derby hat, a ruptured water-boiler, a bicycle frame, whiskey-bottle shards, coils of elevator cable, parts of an antiquated projection

> machine, tire fragments, dry branches, a broken ladder, a cracked porcelain basin, a tangle of barbed-wire, aged and crumpled newspapers, burlap sacks, screens from long-decayed doors, rotten boards, and that last symbol of all ephemeral art, a dunghill.

Riches to ruin in the blink of an eye. It's a real lesson in enjoying it while you have it. I have to admit, here, that the description of the ruins has a lot in common with descriptions of my office. Here's William Whitworth in *The New Yorker:*

> Joe's office is even less like other offices than his television show is like other television shows. It has a quality that goes beyond mere grime and disorder. If it were a person, it would be a bum.

Let me interrupt to say that this bum of an office is the alter ego of the show itself, which is coffee-table neat. If my *show* were a person, it would be a banker. But let's go on—

> On the right as you enter Joe's office is his famous desk. The desk has photographs and magazine clippings taped to its front, and its top is stacked more than a foot high with unopened mail, bulging manila envelopes, photographs, magazines, sheet music, plastic spoons, empty coffee containers, reels of movie film, posters, record albums, demo records, newspapers, books, and unsigned contracts detailing schemes for easy money.

(Before going on, let me quibble about those empty coffee containers. Dick Roffman, a member of my "brain trust," maintains that they're *not* empty, they're half full. Ordering coffee is a way of asking people to stay, or getting somebody out on an errand, or avoiding moments of inactivity. The coffee usually has too much sugar and cream for most people to cope with, especially cold. Cleaning those things up is a delicate matter. Continuing—)

> Lined up facing the desk are five chairs, a nickel-candy machine that dispenses pistachio nuts, and an ancient console-model Edison phonograph. Two of the chairs are filled with envelopes and newspapers, and two more chairs are usually occupied by Joe's aging messenger boys, Happy the Clown and Pop, nattering away at each other like old ladies but ready for action in their felt hats.

As time goes by, details change. Messengers come and go, we've moved a couple of times, and, as Johnson said (not Howard, Lyndon, Van, or Andrew, but Samuel), "Three removes equal a fire." Any list of the items in my office is necessarily out of date after a move. Whitworth has the basic furnishings catalogued—

> A narrow patch of concrete between the desk on one side and the Edison and the various knees on the other is the only standing room in the office. The rest of the floor space is taken up by a jungle-gym assemblage of tall metal and wooden shelves, stacks of cardboard boxes, a table, and three filing cabinets. The sort of debris that covers the desk also covers the shelves, the table, the radiator, and the tops of the filing cabinets, and spills out onto the floor here and there. The filing cabinets are jammed so full of envelopes and folders, fanned out like a hand of jumbo playing cards, that the drawers will close only halfway.

I must interject that we have a method of thinning the files that is effective if not up to the standards of the IRS or Peter Drucker. Our visitors are constantly shifting magazines and press releases to unearth their own packages that have been buried by other visitors shifting magazines and press releases to find *theirs*. It's sort of a lending library of junk mail. In the process, they usually spy something of interest and manage to file it at the bottom of their pile, and remove it on departure. In this way we are spared a Malthusian calamity of printed matter. There is no guard to check anyone at the door, but I have found that most people are honest enough to avoid taking anything they suspect I value, and most people are also interested in *new* magazines rather than old ones. But I think I've lost quite a lot of memorabilia because some people think anything old is fair game. Bette Midler, if you're reading this, give me back some of my sheet music; on second thought, maybe it's serving a better purpose in your hands. To conclude Whitworth's catalog, which is a model for writers of the auction houses:

> Beached atop one of the filing cabinets is a television set that won't last much longer. When it's turned on every morning for Joe's show, dim, ghostly images swim across its screen, speaking in muffled voices. On the walls, which are gray and peeling, there are thirty or forty photographs, including ones of Rudolph Valentino, Frank Sinatra, Eddie Cantor, a Hupmobile, Shirley Temple, Al Jolson, a lady midget, Alfred E. Neuman, Iris the Body, Joe with Kate Smith, Joe with Jimmy Durante, and Joe with Tony Curtis.

And right there is a pretty good description of the kind of mix I would like to have on the show, which I think of as a candy store where giant chocolate confections sit side by side with hard candy. Or a state fair where oversize carrots star with exhibits about the moon walks. I used to read about the old New England trade fairs, organized by something called the Berkshire Agricultural Society (almost everything produced in those days had something to do with the farm). The announcement for the first fair put on by that group started this way:

> We take the liberty to recommend to farmers to select and prepare prime animals for exhibition, also for manufacturers to exhibit their best cloth, etc., etc., for inspection and sale. . . . Innocent recreation will be permitted, but everything tending to immorality will be discountenanced.

(Not a bad description of my ground rules, in fact.)

And from those early fairs came horse races and circuses, for people wanted entertainment as well as a display of wares. Moreover, the dual purpose of the fairs generally created two factions—those who wanted to restrict the fairs to products of the farm and factory, and those who wanted to cater to the tastes of the public, which was starved for amusement—and hence an interesting balance of events for the people who attended.

Getting the right mix isn't a matter of pitting people against each other; it's a matter of balance. You do the same thing when you arrange a dinner party. Except,

I hasten to add, your audience is yourselves. How would you change your guest list if you knew that the whole thing was being taped to be played back for future guests? The people can be different in style and tastes and social situation and age, and still balance each other by having something to say on a common theme.

I mentioned before how Mrs. Babe Ruth was the focus of one of our liveliest and most stirring interviews. At the tail end of that show, I brought a young couple on who seemed to have nothing at all to do with either baseball or nostalgia. Friends told me I was crazy. They were on the show to plug a demonstration bicycle ride through Central Park the following Sunday, to show that the time had come to protect the growing number of cyclists. I wanted that couple to have a few minutes, *with* Mrs. Babe Ruth, for two reasons. First, I was their last chance for some kind of publicity—they needed my help. Second, I thought this earnest young couple would give us a change of pace. I won't say I was right—Who's to say what might have happened otherwise?—but I do know that we discovered that Mrs. Ruth and the cyclists had one great thing in common. They were both believers in demonstrating, or otherwise taking action, to effect changes in our life style. Clare Ruth put her name and her familiar face on the line for little league baseball and many other causes. Only a few brief sentences were exchanged between them, but this chance meeting brought the conversation up to the present and gave the whole show a gentle ending.

They talk, in the trade, about the last two or three

minutes of a talk show as "Siberia." That's when a host has two or three guests waiting in the wings, to be slipped onto the couch for a brief bit of exposure before the final sign-off. The poor wretches barely get their names out, they shake hands with the stars sitting next to them who have been performing for a half hour or more, and that's it. I prefer to have my "Siberia," if there is such a thing on my show, up front. I don't feel I have to sock my viewers in the teeth with a lineup of superstars (even when I have them!). I don't mind beginning slowly, perhaps with a brand-new face, and letting him or her earn the right to continue. What it comes down to is that it's not a performance my viewers want—they want an interesting interlude.

**Come on! Television isn't life and death!** It's funny, or moving, or educational at times, but mostly it's just companionship, like a good book, or a cigar.

Of course, television now is for the most part in the hands of conglomerates, and the dollar sign is evident in everything conglomerates touch. The game of getting to the top of the ratings and outselling your competitors in the same time slot has become something of a spectator sport; columnists eagerly report what shows are being scuttled, what big advertisers are switching networks, and what new contracts the trendy superstars are signing. I'm a holdout against such trends. I know some people accuse me of being an anachronism, but though I'm not leading any crusade, I'll say it plainly for anyone who is interested: Super-slick television will kill itself, just as super-slick baseball will choke on Astroturf and shortstops who carry briefcases to the clubhouse. I'd rather deal with the human race than the rating race. And that's not because the ratings are unkind to me; they're not. I'm usually number one in my time spot among local (non-network) channels.

Three or four years ago I had Otto Preminger and actress Jennifer O'Neil on the same show. She was promoting a John Wayne movie being released just then. Jennifer had made her start in *Summer of '42*, and was the kind of talent I knew Preminger had hired in the past. They got to talking on the show, and Otto blurted out, "You're just the one I need for a movie I'm casting, *Such Good Friends*." She got the part. I should've charged them both an agent's fee. But these things happen mostly because you *don't* plan them.

Of course, I strike out occasionally, too—if you consider it a strike-out (I'm not so sure I do) when the conversation never really gets under way, or when my "discoveries" don't get discovered right away. I hope against hope. Does the world need another young rock and roll singer? I've tried to show the world Sunny Leigh. Does the world need a concert pianist who tries to interpret classical music in a livelier way? I've tried to show the world Nina Deutch's new album. With or without me, these and hundreds of other talented people who come into our conversations are going to make their mark. And I hope *they* put everything they have into it.

Sometimes when the magic doesn't happen by itself, you have to make it happen. There was a furniture manufacturer on once who specialized in one-word answers. There are all sorts of things that can be explored about the manufacture of furniture, but this gentleman thought he should confine himself to what *he* did. No one else on the couch had any interest in his furniture. I was grasping at straws. Finally I thought I saw a way to cut through the Red Sea of yawning silence.

"How do they make piano legs?" I inquired mysteriously.

"On a lathe."

"Why do all the women in the world detest piano legs?" I persisted.

"Because all the men do," he said with gusto, and I had broken through. He had found himself. He had suddenly seen that he didn't have to be so all-fired serious about it. We then had a spirited discussion—of legs.

Trivial question: What President of the United States once published a 38-page book, in office, that sold like wildfire? I've said something in this chapter about my feeling for what my work is and what I should do with my work. That realization didn't come from schooling or from psychiatrists or from meditation. It came as a bonus after many years of work. I read something about that feeling in one of my old second-hand books. I went back to it, the 38-page wonder, and saw it all there—

> It is a very wholesome and regenerating change which a man undergoes when he "comes to himself." It is not only after periods of recklessness or infatuation, when he has played the spendthrift or the fool, that a man comes to himself. He comes to himself after experiences

> of which he alone may be aware: when he has left off being wholly preoccupied with his own powers and interests and with every petty plan that centers in himself; when he has cleared his eyes to see the world as it is, and his own true place and function in it.
>
> It is a process of disillusionment. The scales have fallen away. He sees himself soberly, and knows under what conditions his powers must act, as well as what his powers are. . . . It is a process of disillusionment, but it disheartens no soundly made man. It brings him into a light which guides instead of deceiving him; a light which does not make the way look cold to any man whose eyes are fit for use in the open, but which shines wholesomely, rather upon the obvious path, like the honest rays of the frank sun, and makes traveling both safe and cheerful.

Give or take a phrase or two, that is a fair statement of the process of recognizing how you fit in to the larger conversation of the world. The sentiment is Woodrow Wilson's; the book is *When a Man Comes to Himself.*

# Twenty

# Xenophobia

X-rays and lasers will never replace moonlight and roses, for the fact is that we're more comfortable with things we understand, and no amount of thinking about it will alter the chemistry of our reactions to the world about us. There's a fifty-cent word that means having a fear or hatred of anything strange or foreign: *xenophobia*. A bright man once told me that it is one of the few words in any language that can mean two opposite things, because in Greek, *xenos* can mean either "friend" or "stranger." On second thought, maybe they're not opposite ideas at all.

But I see this happen every day in my job: People get angry about things they don't understand, things that are foreign to them. Once I had Stella Stevens and

Anita Bryant on the same panel. Miss Stevens had just made a splash in the news by being one of the first serious actresses to pose in the nude for *Playboy* magazine. Anita Bryant was already well known as a defender of virtue and of the dignity of the family. (Notice how just *stating* the latter description tends nowadays to draw jeers from most of us. We're afraid of anyone who takes it upon himself, or herself, to tell us anything about morality. Maybe that's because morality itself is something foreign to our society, or maybe it's because someone who sincerely believes he or she knows what virtue is appears strange to us.) In any case, at the sight of each other these two lovely women began to bare their claws. I had hoped they could keep the morality issue in the background, but no, that's what they wanted to talk about. The serene, friendly atmosphere I like to cultivate had gone out the window as they went for the jugular. Since I don't consider myself a referee, I decided once again to open that safety valve, the well-timed commercial. During "recess," I was able to disengage the pair and suggest a new topic, and after that, politeness prevailed. But the conviction remained that these two women represented great numbers of people who would never be able to understand another person's point of view.

Virginia Graham told me an even more extreme story of two panel members at each other's throats. In the middle of a newspaper strike, when she had had difficulty keeping up with the latest Hollywood gossip, she inadvertently scheduled on the same show both the wife and the mistress of the same actor. A few days before the show was to go on, the wife informed

Virginia just who the other woman was, that she had even found the mistress in bed with her husband and just about throttled her. The gossip mills had spread the story around town, but it hadn't reached Virginia's producers. "I gave the wife three stiff drinks," Miss Graham explained, "and tried to convince her that going on the show would be to her great advantage. She would make the other woman look like the fool she was, and her husband would then get the message—what a fool he had been." And that's exactly what happened. To this day she rates it as one of her best shows. What I like about the story is the way it neatly illustrates how to handle a situation in which fear and hatred seem to be impossible barriers: You give the participants a motive for overcoming the barriers. For again, the simple fact is, we'd all prefer not to explore the new, the untried, the strange—unless we've got a very compelling reason unrelated to the situation.

Recall how great discoveries, or great achievements, are made. Columbus set out in search of a route to the East—because the route around Africa had become too dangerous. We put a man on the moon because John F. Kennedy saw it as the psychological counter to Russian advances. To this day, incidentally, there are people in this country who don't believe a man ever did walk on the moon; it's too foreign to their way of thinking. It's easier for them to believe that it was all a giant hoax of the government.

Ordinarily I'm not interested in the paraphernalia of the broadcast business; perhaps the mechanics of it all frightens me, like X-rays and lasers. But there's one little item that fascinates me *because I have another motive for studying it.* It's the magnetic tape head, and my motive is the fact that one of my favorite performers had a little-known role in its development, Bing Crosby.

Right after the Second World War the broadcast industry was still laboring with the problem of "dubbing," their programs on records so that they could be rebroadcast later for other parts of the country. Radio shows had to cut seventeen hours of programs every day on discs, sometimes two or three copies for shows that were aired at various times. Music and variety programs especially suffered from a loss of fidelity from one copy to the next. And Bing Crosby, whose Philco Hour was on the ABC network at the time, was concerned that the recordings were full of interference and had little in common with the quality of the actual performance.

Enter Harold Lindsay. He saw that wire recorders didn't have the potential for high fidelity the industry needed. He was familiar with German work in the field of tape recording. He got the attention of the legendary Alexander Poniatoff, who was then head of a motor manufacturing firm called Ampex Electric and Manufacturing Company. Ampex. The company gave Lindsay the go-ahead.

On the designated date, the industry executives arrived for a demonstration. They showed the playback head. . . . It worked! Everybody was elated. Fortunately, no one wanted to see the recording head, which was nonexistent. Now the contracts poured in, but there was no money for production. Enter Bing Crosby again. The crooner sent an unsolicited check in time to get the program off the ground. On April 25, 1948, twenty machines started operating to make network radio what it is today. But now television was here. And so was Ampex.

Success stories like this are usually told to show how inconspicuous little events can sometimes lead to great achievements. I like to point out the motivations behind those achievements. **People don't venture into strange territory unless something is nagging at them to take the leap.** Fear keeps us away from moving into the unknown. City people shun the country; suburbanites think there are sinister elements lurking in every alley of the city. (Though Arthur Conan Doyle had Mr. Holmes say, in "The Adventure of the Copper Beeches," "It is my belief, Watson, founded upon my experience, that the lowest and vilest alleys in London do not present a more dreadful record of sin than does the smiling and beautiful countryside.")

**To break the barriers of xenophobia, you have to realize that the other person is just as wary of you as you are of him or her.** If that is true, then it would follow that it would help matters if you could see yourself as that other person is seeing you—that old prescription for success that everybody talks about—find out what you do that might make others more wary of you, or less so.

How are you ever going to do that? After all, people have been trying since the beginning of time. Well, I'm suggesting a technique.

First you remember—and be objective about it, now—how your voice sounds on a tape recorder, or what points that caricaturist chose to bring out in his drawing of you. Use anything else available, a home movie, perhaps, to get an idea of how you come across.

Then picture yourself, at this very moment, sitting

across the room from where you are, watching yourself read. Extend that picture to the activity you are likely to engage in tomorrow: walking to work, having lunch with a friend, talking business with someone you scarcely know, explaining the meaning of a word to a child, and watch yourself doing those things. Pretend you're a hidden camera looking at yourself. But you have to think now about something that's going to happen tomorrow, because when it actually happens you'll be too close to it to see yourself realistically. Imagining how you appear, how you come across to others, should help you modify your behavior in a way that reduces the other person's wariness of you. **I rehearse to be able to meet strangers. I watch myself from a distance.**

Another exercise: Next time you're talking to someone face to face, look that person squarely in the eyes and try to see yourself in those eyes. But you have to do these exercises frequently to notice any change in your behavior. Get in the habit of watching yourself, and you'll avoid an awful lot of gauche behavior. You may even discover that you're starting to like yourself better.

Jerry Colonna had a once-in-a-lifetime opportunity to see himself as others do, and he found out that he was funnier than he had given himself credit for. Until that day, this great comedian had always felt he was living in Bob Hope's shadow.

The industry had decided to honor him with a gala affair at Sardi's. Hundreds of guests in evening clothes assembled at the appointed hour, but Jerry was nowhere in sight. Vincent Sardi decided to take matters into his own hands. He tracked down Colonna at the NBC studios and found to his horror that the guest of honor was trapped in a taping session that was running an hour overtime. He was going to have to stall somehow. Then he spotted a professional mimic in the audience, and a light bulb flashed in a little round circle over his head. After a hurried costume change, there was Jerry Colonna, mustache and all, on stage. The impromptu performance went on for nearly half an hour, at the end of which only Vincent Sardi noticed the real Mr. Colonna doubled up in laughter at the back of the room.

**Meeting strangers becomes especially fearful if you have to meet people whose life style is obviously very different from yours.** Old–young, rich–poor, socially prominent–nouveau riche. And in the entertainment business, especially, those clashes are intensified when one of the parties is trying to land a job. Stars just past their prime have to work very hard to make the grade when meeting their younger booking agents.

There's a fine story on this subject to tell about Walter Hampden. You old-timers may rightly associate Walter with his definitive portrayal of Cyrano de Bergerac. (That was no small feat. John Barrymore himself had tried his hand at it. José Ferrer carried it off in fine style for the following generation. The playwright, Edmund Rostand, isn't known for much else, but he excited the aspirations of the greatest actors of several generations for this key part.) Mr. Hampden impressed the whole world of the theater with his sensitivity; the lights dim, he reads with increasing feeling the letter that is supposedly from Christian, but which the heroine senses from his reading really expresses his own feelings. Now see Mr. Hampden in the offices of David Susskind many years later to discuss a possible TV special based on his old role. He is confronted with the paraphernalia of the modern broadcasting corporation. The well-manicured receptionist inquires, "Who are you?"

"I'm Walter Hampden, an actor."

"What have you done?" she inquires brusquely, having judged him a has-been instead of an actor with a string of successes on the American stage.

Without hesitation, he answers, "To whom?"

# Twenty-one

*

# Cowboys Are the Real Thing

I lament the impermanence of things and the loss of straightness and trueness in our lives. The wood frames of the ghost towns of the West were impermanent, but there was a straightness there just the same. The wood dripped water. Green grain split. The rutted main streets were peopled by men like John Wayne and Gary Cooper and Buck Jones. Straightness.

What if this new generation never sees those "B" movies that you and I saw on Saturday mornings? What if they go to the circus and find out it's just Madison Square Garden or the Civic Auditorium awash with tumblers, impressarios, and jazz bands trying to imitate *The Entrance of the Gladiators*? Where will they find their models of fairness and majesty?

Do you remember the sawdust, the smell of unwashed animals? Under a real big top, a canvas tent instead of dusty concrete, we stomped the wooden planks they called seats and huddled together silently as trapeze artists, swarthy and heavily bandaged in wool, flew through the air over us. All clowns were Emmet Kelly, and Barnum and Bailey and Ringling and Pollack were names of magicians, not promoters. The magic was that we were part of the circus, we weren't isolated from it behind a screen. And I would like to say we used to be part of cowboy movies, too. The cowboy flicks have a reality that makes them endure while drawing-room comedies, gangster epics, and historical romances fade. At least that's what I'm going to argue.

I'm talking about the "B" Westerns, in which the heroes were also accomplished stuntmen, like Kermit Maynard. They really did jump off roofs into the saddle, dive for a gun across a splintered wooden floor while the fuse on a keg of gunpowder hissed in the background, and grab an overhanging tree limb at full gallop. I remember Tim McCoy and Buck Jones especially, because they were still at their peak, in the late thirties, when I started to frequent the neighborhood movie house.

Theoretically we all knew that there were modern cities in the Southwest and on the Coast, but we pictured the real West as a vast stretch of badlands in between those cities, where indians still ambushed wagon trains and the horse was the only form of transportation. Those films were current events! There was little in them to suggest a bygone era—to put it in television terms, to us the action was "live."

Violence, however, wasn't pursued for its own sake. Bandits crumpled under a fusillade of .45 slugs, but the camera didn't linger on the wound. It was a reasonable convention: It was left to our imagination to know what a bullet does to the flesh, just as we didn't have to see a close-up of sexual intercourse to know what went on after the hero and heroine rode into the sunset.

That's the key—imagination. It sounds inconsistent; the dirt and the saddle blankets wet with sweat and the moss on the granite boulders were real, but sex and violence were sanitized. Yet it wasn't just a puritanical cop-out. Those filmmakers realized, perhaps unconsciously, that sex and violence were extremely sensitive weapons to introduce into such a young medium. Their explosiveness would overpower the delicate nature of the Western plots. For the early Westerns were essentially morality plays from the Middle Ages recast on a great frontier of human exploration.

Maybe we're more blasé these days. Certainly the Victorian code of dress, language, and behavior still had hold in the thirties. But I lean to the view that the bikini and the prevalence of the four-letter word haven't really altered our sensitivity about sex. We may see more of the epidermis of the opposite sex, and say more about the sex act, but our natural urges are still very much a mystery to us. Read "Dear Abby" or the true-confession magazines and see if the human comedy isn't still in reruns.

In grammar school we acted out scenes from our favorite radio programs and cowboy movies. I remember the thrill of playing the Lone Ranger during recess, with an Italian friend as Tonto. With a handkerchief tied around his forehead he was just dark enough to bear some resemblance to a "redskin," and nobody minded that I was shorter than he. They *imagined* the rest. What do they play at during recess nowadays? Where is the reality our kids can sink themselves into?

The producers of those "B" Westerns often took it upon themselves to change the endings, especially if the script called for the hero to die in the final reel. They abhorred unhappy endings the way nature abhors a vacuum, and for the same reason. Movies were the vitamins of the psyche, booster shots against the depression of the Great Depression. And a hero who might have potential for a sequel could no more be allowed to die than the protagonist of a comic strip.

Did you ever notice the stern, fatherly look of the cowboy heroes? McCoy and Jones, Tom Mix and William S. Hart, Gene Autry and William Boyd all seemed to have faces of granite and years of experience etched in their foreheads. They were solid men, and they dressed in the leather and embroidery that were the grey flannel suits of the range. About the first youthful face to come along was Buster Crabbe's. Apparently we pictured cowboys as men, not boys; the baby-faced Bob Livingston didn't catch on, while the formidable Johnny Mack Brown wowed 'em. As the thirties ended, another kind of face came to the center of the stage: the sensitive, thoughtful, *vulnerable* hero. There were Randolph Scott and Joel McCrea, Fred MacMurray, Robert Taylor, John Wayne, Gary Cooper. Cooper's tentative smile and graceful bearing marked him as the loner on a lifelong search for meaning rather than the patriarch at the head of the table. And their clothes also became softer, less formal. The string ties were loosened to reveal Adam's apples, and supple, tassled jackets replaced the tailored shirts with button-down pockets.

But the women! What fresh, sparkling faces! Except for the oft-miscast Calamity Jane, the ladies took second fiddle in the script, but gave us a picture of female beauty that I suspect hasn't been equaled in the movies since. If you don't believe me, or can't trust your memory, take a look at some of the old stills. For one thing, young actresses got their first chance in Westerns; they all seem to have that first blush of womanhood. Marsha Hunt in *Desert Gold,* Fay Wray in *The Conquering Horde,* Jean Arthur in *The Plainsman,* Joan Bennett in *The Texans,* Laraine Day in *Arizona Legion,* an effervescent Rita Hayworth in *Rebellion,* and, of course, Jeannette MacDonald in *Rose Marie*. . . . The hairdos were the stylish thirties close-crop, the eyes were anything but sultry, the form was boyish, and the manner was farm fresh. Is that bad?

The big, serious Westerns of the fifties and sixties would change all this, and push what I call the cowboy Westerns into a limbo of low budgets and very, very Grade-B performances. *High Noon, Shane, Across the Wide Missouri,* and *Bad Day at Black Rock* were typical of the new direction in Western action. Gone was the convention of implied, not explicit, violence and sex. Gone were the easy formulas that inevitably led to happy endings. And here's my point: The productions were now so flawless, so perfectly staged, that the reality was drained out of them. You knew that Kirk Douglas and Burt Lancaster couldn't really ride hell-bent for leather in *Gunfight at the OK Corral,* even though Kirk Douglas is tougher off the screen than he is on. What pleased me most in these "A" Westerns were the elements of the old "B's" which crept through, such as the towering heroics of Gary Cooper in *High Noon*.

My specialty is really the silents, not the talkies. I guess it's the human, obvious, almost amateurish quality of those pioneer films and the early Westerns that means so much to me. In fact, the most interesting of all the eras of film, to me at any rate, was that period when the talkies took over but the new technology was still in an experimental stage. We knew they had to have a microphone somewhere to pick up the dialogue. And the microphones were big and clumsy. Where were they hidden? Every now and then you could spot one behind the potted plant or under the bed. The heroine would be gazing into her lover's eyes and whispering sweet nothings—to that mike bobbing from the ceiling. We were watching talented people in the throes of a creative breakthrough. We were witnessing human beings, not actors.

Nowadays we go to university theaters to see "experimental" films, to get the same kind of thrill of discovery. I've lectured on quite a few campuses about this very subject: Every film festival honors up-and-coming filmmakers for doing exactly what people like Mack Sennett and King Vidor and D. W. Griffith did at the beginning of their careers. But somehow we sense they had more at stake than the new breed. They certainly had more fun.

Movies today have submerged the individual in a

sea of special effects. The strong characters, the heroic faces are missing. There's Redford and Pacino. James Bacon says that Streisand has been the only real female star, in the best sense of the word, in the last ten years. Let me tell two stories, one old, one new, to make my point.

At the climax of one of his great old silents, *Hard Luck,* Buster Keaton had to dive off a sixty-foot-high platform. He was his own stunt man, of course, as were the three other all-time greats of silent comedy, Harold Lloyd, Harry Langdon, and Charlie Chaplin. The trick in this stunt was that he had to miss the pool and crash into the marble tiling, at least a papier-mâché imitation of marble that would allow him to sink inexplicably into the earth. The stunt itself was going to be no mean feat, but Keaton got the shock of his life when he discovered, on looking down, that the imitation was so carefully done that he couldn't tell the difference between it and the real tile. Before he could decide what to do, a gust of wind pitched him over the edge and he made a midair evaluation of hard and soft surfaces. Ringed by an impression of bathing beauties, he plunged safely through the paper. To film buffs today, it's just another zany Keaton finale: After a swift passage of several years, he emerges from the tiling with a Chinese wife and their brood. But the terror of a possibly fatal accident was accepted as a way of life by these pioneers.

Few people remember that Mabel Normand also did her own stunts, diving from the crow's nest of a ship, in one case, for the benefit of Mack Sennett. (I'm afraid I have to report that far too few people even remember

Mabel Normand.) But my second story concerns an actor whose concern for reality has gone largely unnoticed even in today's world of the press agent.

In *Three Days of the Condor,* Robert Redford played a resourceful CIA man who survived a series of murder attempts. The close-ups were vital to the plot, and there are not too many doubles who can successfully look like Robert Redford. So he had to handle all the rock-'em sock-'em stuff on his own. He and his diabolical adversary, Hank Garrett, fought it out in one sequence that lasted about two hours and left them both with cuts and bruises. Finally Redford was scripted to be grabbed for a judo throw, but he came in a foot low and was caught on the nose by a hard right that was aimed for his chest. No one knew it at the time, but Redford's nose was broken. Still he went on through another couple of hours of the fight sequence. Several weeks later, Redford casually mentioned to Garrett that he had broken his nose in the *Condor* fight scene. I asked Garrett if this was a typical Redford performance, or some kind of carefully contrived bit of one-upmanship. "It's a side of Redford few people know," he answered. "The guy was offering me a part in his next movie, and he thought this was just a funny anecdote to relate. The guy's real, on camera or off."

That gave me a lift. The stars will always be around. The way I see it, Redford is a cowboy at heart.

# Twenty-two

*

# Questions Without Answers

Query: Why do people always want an answer? Do they feel the purpose of life is to answer questions, so that at the end they will pass the final examination and get their reward? Half the world's problems, I sometimes think, are the result of trying to wring answers from people and events where no answers are possible.

I vaguely remember a scene from one of Shaw's plays where a Christian is being questioned by an emperor about the wisdom of being a martyr. The emperor is dumbfounded by the young man's willingness to die for an apparently obscure cause. He asks for an explanation of the Christian faith to justify such an irrational act. The young man answers in words to this effect: If the cause was small enough of a matter to be explainable, it wouldn't be worth dying for. What was the play and what were the exact lines? Now there's a question that *can* be answered.

One of the nicest pieces of advice I ever heard about questions and answers between husband and wife came from Bing and Kathy Crosby on one of our shows. "Sure we have problems," Bing said. "Some of 'em can be solved, some can't. With some difficulties you don't try to resolve anything—you dissolve them by ignoring them."

Put yourself in my position for a moment. Every day I see a stream of people who have answers to problems. They are writers who know what's wrong with the post office, or actors who have the latest word on self-fulfillment, or inventors who have discovered a way to end wars with games. That's all I hear all day—answers, answers, answers. I long for the occasional visitor who just wants to sit and dream, to stand in the presence of life's difficulties and wonder about them. The rush to find answers even where there *are* answers is fraught with danger.

**Too many people think they have the answer to their problems, and their answer is that they're doomed to failure.** They have a need to be rejected. I'm supposed to be a nice guy who "puts anybody on the show," but I have to turn down 5,000 people a month. Sometimes I see someone who is particularly self-destructive, and I try to turn him around by giving him a spot on the show. As a result, I am besieged on all sides by people who have answers of their own as well as by those whose answer is the Joe Franklin lifeline.

**You have to be prepared to have your questions go unanswered, too.** You may ask an embarrassing question by mistake. You may ask too great a favor, and not know it. And you have to have a followup if your question is taken rhetorically. **But the biggest question of all, which remains unanswered as far as I know, is, How do you reach people?** What makes a work of art meaningful to other people? Is it just because it pleases us? Or are you on firmer ground if you avoid your own sentiments and try to please others? Should you undertake research to find out what pleases others? Or should you trust your own ties to humanity?

I have always followed my own instincts; what I liked in old records and old movies and Tarzan and Tom Mix was what I thought a good many other people liked. **Everything I have written I have written for my own tastes.** The questions I have asked have been questions I didn't know the answers to, and wanted answers for. Sometimes we deceive ourselves: Our questions are really only attempts to reaffirm ourselves, to build up our own egos, and we have to subdue some of those tendencies to keep in touch with the rest of humanity. Or, if shyness is the problem, we have to overcome it, just as much as egomania; it depends on what we start with.

A. E. Housman reported that he liked a pint of beer to loosen up his conservative nature. Samuel Taylor Coleridge used drugs when writing, and the images in *Kubla Khan* seem to have gained as a result. Charlie Chaplin at first was a caricature of himself. He was indeed the little tramp, so self-conscious he couldn't face the cameras. Gene Fowler tells about his transformation in a film called *Making a Living*—

Mabel Normand was to have played the lead in this picture. It did not help matters when she sought to overcome Chaplin's timidity by taunts, which only lashed his fears. The consequence was that he flatly refused to appear before the camera with her. Minta Durfee was substituted for Mabel.

Work begun, Chaplin miraculously shed his phobia. He began to ask pertinent questions. Nothing escaped him. His years of experience in the ancient art of pantomime gave him immense advantages in the field of pictorial expression. And now, while the picture was being taken, he startled everyone who had thought him so terribly backward and almost neurotically diffident. He had *ideas.*

**"He began to ask pertinent questions." That's the beginning of becoming human.** Sometimes I sense that the questions I ask don't have answers, but they do bring up thoughts that the respondent wants to talk about. Jane Wyman and the late Rosalind Russell were promoting an arthritis telethon over WOR-TV a few years ago, and made use of my show to focus on the event. I realized that the cause was good; I shouldn't take advantage of any of the many issues in the background of both these grand actresses to titillate our viewers. But I also knew what the human-interest equation was. I felt that Jane Wyman wanted to capture the attention of her fans. I suspected how her fans felt about her former husband, Ronald Reagan, who was, at the time, just about the most prominent man in conservative politics. He was in the limelight; she had been somewhat out of it. I introduced the whole subject with some tentative questions about her feelings about politics. She didn't hesitate. It was almost a purgative. We talked for ninety percent of the show about the old days with Ronnie and the Hollywood crowd. By the end of the show it was obvious this wasn't just an advertisement for some other appearance. It was a real conversation. May I tell you how important this is when the advertisement does come? No audience wants ten percent entertainment followed by ninety percent plug.

Some questions deserve not to be answered. Sex and race are sensitive topics for discussion, in which questions must be delicately posed. Believe it or not, I have seen interviewers ask Sammy Davis, Jr., if he ever wanted to be white. What kind of an answer do they expect, except something that might put the respondent ill at ease? But there is a school of broadcast interviewers who insist that everything be provocative and bright and abrasive. The hope behind it is that something newsworthy might result. The guest might become angry or have a heart attack on camera.

Questions can be outrageous, of course, or illogical, as I have insisted already. Not only does the general public think in a nonlinear way, poets and writers and politicians do, too. They do because they pose questions to themselves and answer them for themselves as they go along, without knowing in advance where they're going.

**Surprises always work out for the best in the end, even when they start out unpleasantly.**

Recently I arranged for theater tickets for a couple who were working to promote a cultural exchange.

They arrived at the theater to discover there were no tickets in their name. They called me the next morning to register their chagrin, in a most polite way, under the circumstances. I was aghast! I called the theater to discover they did not, indeed, have the tickets I had arranged. In my haste, I had called the wrong theater. So two tickets had gone begging and two people had gone without their eagerly awaited entertainment. I spent the next half hour making it up. This time I got six tickets, and had them sent by messenger to the couple's hotel. They were for the next-best show in town. I called to make sure the tickets arrived. I hoped the extra tickets might work for friends. To my surprise (no, I expect things like this, à la Mr. Frost) I discovered that the couple really wanted to see my second choice, and that they had two other couples coming to visit them that evening. It would be a joyous occasion! I was about to say, "You're gonna have a big, big surprise"—but they already had! I was going to say, "It's better this way, much better," but the words fell flat before I could get them out. I even surprised myself.

One final answer: Shaw's play mentioned at the beginning of this chapter is *Androcles and the Lion*. And one final question: Have you read this far? You're wonderful!

# Twenty-three
*
# I Love You

It don't mean a thing if it ain't got that swing. That's why husbands and other lovers don't feel they should have to say I love you at the drop of every handkerchief. But, say I, they're way off base.

Remember the old story about the Scotsman who wanted to send his fondest regards to his beloved? His ten-word telegram read, "I love you, I love you, I love you, Sincerely." Whenever we try to express our deepest emotions, something always seems to intrude. It may be just our culture. It's difficult in our society for two men to hug each other without feeling a little funny, except that, ironically, football players can do it on a crucial touchdown. But a handshake is as far as most feel free to go in showing their emotions. And wives can't understand why those three little words are sometimes so hard for men to utter. I confess I find it troublesome.

I say I love you all day long, sometimes to total strangers. And the words aren't diluted to meaninglessness by being repeated. There are just a handful of phrases in English (or any other language, I suppose) that have magic. The magical property of these three little words is that they pack such a wallop they can't be overused. They also act like something of a lie-detector test. When you say them your heart begins to pump a little faster; your throat tightens. And these things translate, via body language, into a message like a dispatch from Reuters.

So I imagine that even at the other end of a telephone, there is a flash of recognition of some sort of feeling when I say, "I love ya, sweetheart." That's why I believe that you shouldn't worry about overuse of those three little words. Underuse is the more obvious and prevalent danger.

Now, if I am nothing else I am a practical man. I like to get to some tangible conclusion. And I know that all the preaching and posturing in the world about telling your wife (or your husband) you love her (him) won't do any good unless you are told *how* to do it as well as *to* do it. Therefore I have devised a list of ways of building up to saying I love you. Here follows the Joe Franklin Ten-Point Program for Expressing Love Without Actually Uttering the Word.

1. *Use all the words you can think of except those you*

*read in poetry classes.* Remember that great scene in *The Owl and the Pussycat* when Barbra Streisand leans across the bar in her apartment and announces casually to her male friend, "Do ya wanna mess around?" Tell her you like her, admire her, want to be around her, need her, have a hankering for her. But you know better words than I do.

2. *Etch her name into your life in some way.* (Dear Reader, Remember that I am writing from a man's point of view. I trust by now that I need not constantly translate everything into the female viewpoint. You can do that better than I can.) Give her a special code name. It could be an animal, like a toad, or a tree, or anything with a vague connection with your loved one. Everyone has some special distinction. Eddie Cantor first sang "Ida" (sweet as apple cidah) in tribute to his childhood sweetheart. Twelve years later he married her. And whenever he had the chance, he trotted out that song and dedicated it to her. That was a real song.

3. *Get physical.* Hold hands, smooth out hair, play footsies when out to dinner with friends. Now there's body language that can't be misunderstood. Stroke, as they say in crew.

4. *Get specific.* Say, "Let's do this." Dinner, dancing, moviegoing all come under this heading, but they're not very original. Try something unusual. But it must be something specific. Instead of dinner, send out for sandwiches. Don't think that *what* you do is critical. Think that your doing something *definite* is.

5. *Imitate her.* Don't mimic her, but follow her exam-

ple, her lead. Give tennis a try if she's a buff; let her tell you about ballet.

6. *Write to her.* Write notes, letters, epistles, gospels. Write love poems, if you feel up to it. You'd be surprised how sugary some of the best-known and most-quoted love poems are—even Shakespeare's. It isn't bad to be sugary, just don't be saccharine.

7. *Do it in Macy's window.* Whatever form of expression suits you, do it in front of other people. She secretly wants an audience (and, whether you know it or not, so do you). Don't save expressing yourself for a private moment. It means more to her if you invest it with commitment. (And she assumes it's a commitment for you to show any sign of emotion.)

8. *Overdo it.* Exaggerate it. But not just with words, use gifts, flowers, records. Believe more than you dare to believe. Don't think you're lying without adequate evidence to the contrary. Candy is still candy.

9. *Cook.* That's just an example. But do something that takes some doing on your part. If you're a carpenter, build her a birdhouse. If you paint, paint her.

10. *Be silent.* Don't just blurt out everything that pops into your mind. And restrain your desire to prove everything rationally. Silence works wonders for your thought processes. It also signals her that your waters run deep.

The power of a few well-chosen words, even in the corniest of circumstances, never ceases to astonish me. And next time you're choosing words, consider poetry.

Among the books that I picked up prowling the second-hand stores were many collections of poetry and cracker-barrel advice. Tastes don't change that much. Among the books of poetry I especially liked were those of James Whitcomb Riley, and one poem in particular—

When Lide Married *Him*

When Lide Married *him*—w'y, she had to jes' dee-fy
The whole popilation!—But she never bat' an eye!
Her parents begged, and *threatened*—she must give him
    up—that *he*
Wuz jes' "a common drunkard!"—and he *wuz,*
    appearantly.—
        Swore they'd chase him off the place
        Ef he ever showed his face—
Long after she'd *eloped* with him and *married* him fer
    shore!—
When Lide married *him*, it wuz *"Katy, bar the door!"*

When Lide married *him*—Well! she had to go and be
a *hired girl* in town somewheres—while he tromped
    round to see
What *he* could git that *he* could do,—you might say,
    jes' sawed wood
From door to door!—that's what he done—'cause that
    wuz best he could!
        And the strangest thing, i jing!
        Wuz, he didn't *drink* a thing,—
But jes' got down to bizness, like he someway *wanted*
    to,
When Lide married *him,* like they warned her *not* to
    do!

When Lide married *him*—er, ruther, *had* be'n married
A little up'ards of a year—some feller come and carried
That *hired girl* away with him—a ruther *stylish* feller

In a bran-new green spring-wagon, with the wheels
striped red and yeller:
And he whispered, as they driv
To'rds the country, *"Now we'll live!"*—
And *somepin' else* she *laughed* to hear, though both her
eyes wuz dim,
'Bout *"trustin' Love and Heav'n above,* sence Lide married
*him!"*

Why were both her eyes dim? I couldn't believe the poet meant what he said. The rest of the page was filled out with a photograph of what I thought had to be an Indiana landscape: cows in a meadow, a scrub tree, and two youngsters in farm clothes staring off to a distant river. Was she Lide? She wouldn't run off with that slick city feller, would she? How could a man writing about love be so cynical as to have that dude whisper about trusting love and heaven above as he stole the true love of a reformed drunkard?

Then I saw that last word, *him*. The poet had done everything they taught you not to do in school. Dozens of words italicized. Dashes and exclamation points all over the place. And a sing-song refrain, "Lide married *him*," always with *him* in italics, which seemed pointless. But it was the last *him* that was the punch line. *He* was that rather stylish feller. *He* had made good. *He* carried that hired girl away with him in his flashy wagon. He sure showed them. I know that man; I idolize Lide for throwing in with him.

That poem lives in my mind with the impact of a three-hour wide-screen adventure film. And the happy ending is all the more touching because in the next-to-last scene a villain has appeared on the horizon to tempt that beautiful, trusting girl away. And it looks as if she's a goner, already crying tears of remorse for giving up the fight, when it turns out those are tears of joy because the villain is actually *him,* and no villain at all.

Gee whiz, I want to say, weren't the old songs full of love-talk that we don't have today? And the poetry especially—wasn't it charged with feeling? The rage a few years ago was the photo-caption love story. Beautiful double-black halftones, the full width and depth of the page, of lovers intertwined or a moon rising on a pastoral landscape, were adorned by a few lines of type on the opposite page. I think our imaginations are better than the halftones. I think words suggest more than pictures.

**Saying I love you is not of course reserved for lovers, including married ones. But saying it to others you love is seldom easy.** Children have emotional blocks about telling their parents they love them. Brothers and sisters fear they may be teased if they open up their hearts to each other.

The entertainment business is full of family relationships that the public is unaware of. Jane Fonda must be the daughter of Henry Fonda, but many people never stop to think that Liza Minelli is Judy Garland reborn, until, that is, they see both perform! And on one epic occasion they came up with a performance that illustrated just about all the Joe Franklin Program outlined above.

Liza was starring in her first big role, an off-Broadway production called "Best Foot Forward." Her mother was down in the orchestra seats eating it up.

Liza was making it! Liza launched into one of the show's big songs, "A Little Joint with a Jukebox," and it was all Judy could do to contain herself. Soon she began humming the melody, then mouthing it, and finally singing along. Judy Garland is not the type to soft-pedal a song. Her voice was drowning out her daughter's. The audience didn't take kindly to the performance. They had come to see the daughter of Judy Garland and here was some mimic in the front row spoiling the show. Before the unruly crowd threw the imposter out, Liza called a halt. The theater was hushed.

"Would the young lady auditioning in the audience please hold off for the moment, and come back for the casting call on Tuesday?" she said firmly. And her broad wink also told the audience something. All went smoothly for the rest of the show. Then after the final curtain the woman in the front row ascended the stage to give this favored crowd a rare duet performance of "Over the Rainbow."

How many ways of saying I love you can you count in that episode? How do you suppose the audience said I love you to Judy and Liza?

The adulation that fans have for stars, though, can take quite a different form. And it surely doesn't seem like an expression of love to tear the shirt off someone's back (if all you want is the shirt as a souvenir). The outrages that stars have had to suffer go back to the Charlie Chaplin silent-film era. He was almost decapitated in Paris by a mob of "well-wishers." Mabel Normand also took a goodly share of well-meaning abuse. Then attention turned to popular singers. The bobby-soxers swooned over Frankie and rock and roll stars began wearing breakaway shirts and trousers, like football players. Two of the greatest idols, Marlene Dietrich and Robert Taylor, suffered torture of a subtler nature. Dietrich was often the target of journalists who wanted to pierce the mystery of her elusive sexiness. Taylor was the victim of a publicity story about the hair on his chest: Was it real? Both stars returned the misguided affection of their admirers with a neat ploy. Turning the spotlight on their overly eager fans, they said something like, "Let's not get involved—I may lose my head!"

In that case, they were saying I love you without meaning a word of it. And their fans knew it. But it served the purpose. No, it don't mean a thing if it ain't got that swing, but the words are sweet without the swing, and you can never say I love you too many times.

# Twenty-four

*

# Dream Along with Me

Deny yourself, the philosopher says. I've tried to say something like that in "Don't be *on*." That's in a conversation. But when you're all alone, or, better yet, with friends who know you so well you feel as if you're all alone, you can dream.

You can dream of what you've done, or what you want to do. You can rhapsodize about yourself. You can say to your friends, "It's my turn—let me tell you how good I feel!" I'm doing something like that in writing this book.

TV critics and the people who write profiles for magazines continue to ask me if I couldn't have done something better with my time. They want to know why I didn't take a shot at one of the "hotseats," the network talk shows. Why do I go on year after year, seemingly content with the same format I started with? And I give a lot of answers to these probes: You know, I'm content with what I've got; once a local show goes national and flops, it can never go back to a local show; I like having an audience I can feel out there; and so forth. But H. L. Mencken had a pithier answer, which he wrote to Will Durant to assure the philosopher–historian that he was not wasting his talent continuing to be a newspaperman—

> A cow goes on giving milk all her life, even though what appears to be her self-interest urges her to give gin.

A good many cows dream of giving gin when they should be content with giving milk. I can't get enough of my work. I don't long for new formats. George Jessel has been on my show something like 175 times, and each appearance was a revelation. Then along comes someone like Carol Pearce, to write a profile of me in a magazine published by a well-known TV personality, nominally a competitor. And she says, without prompting—

> Joe has a sexy velvet voice and women are wild about him. . . . Joe's a very special person. A real human being in the world of tinsel and plastic. A *man* in a field that emasculates its performers and turns them into puppets. A person of enormous generosity and warmth, still managing to operate somehow in the marketplaces of the hustlers.

To which all I can say is, But what about my humility? Yes, I love it. *Love* it! Allow me to share my dream with you, to boast a little in front of you, at least while it lasts.

Humility is a matter of relationships. If you have done nothing at all, it's difficult to be humble. If you have accomplished something, you have room to undershoot your idea of yourself.

Joan Fontaine told me a wonderful story on the sub ject of humility. Shortly after her triumph in *Rebecca,* she was invited to dinner at the Goldwyn's. Sam's hilltop residence was the symbol of success to the Hollywood stars; you had really made it when you got that invitation to "come up." She and her husband, Brian Aherne, were prepared for this summit meeting par excellence. They arrived in their finest, fashionably late, only to discover that no other cars had parked in the driveway. To avoid seeming eager, they decided to drive around awhile—but still no one showed up. "Let's go home and check the invitation," Brian suggested. "We must have the wrong day." So they did, but the date and time were right. Now an hour late, they screwed up their courage and made their entrance, only to discover that the Goldwyns were indeed waiting for them—for a dinner alone.

Dream along with me. This is what John J. O'Connor recently wrote in the *New York Times,* about what he calls "the Franklin mix":

> Tonight, amid the standard mix of reruns, possible pilots or a sports event, attention might be paid to a sturdy institution called "The Joe Franklin Show." . . . The Dick Cavetts, the David Frosts, and a host of other luminaries have come and gone with their nightly talk shows, but Joe Franklin has lasted—on different

> channels, at different hours, under different program titles—since he began in October 1953 with Fannie Hurst as one of his guests. One of his most obvious assets is his unabashed enthusiasm. The result is an incredible variety of personalities parading past the show's cameras, from aspiring actors in some Off Off Broadway experiment to established authors hawking their new books. Their egos are nicely inflated by the diminutive Mr. Franklin's inimitable hyperbole, and then they are allowed the luxury of an attractive display of their various talents. The threat of hostile confrontation is nonexistent. Tonight's guests include Janet Gaynor.

John, you're a very smart man. A genius, a *genius*. But about that word *diminutive*. . . .

Let me tell you what makes me feel happy. Not long ago Debbie Reynolds called out of the clear blue sky and asked me to dinner at *her* place. Unbeknownst to me, she has been a regular Joe Franklin watcher and wondered if she could be on the show. Silly girl. Debbie was such a dynamic guest that I offered her a regular spot as "anchor lady," if she ever moved to New York.

Well, now that I've gotten started, let me revel in this dream. Occasionally I would spot Marilyn Monroe in the street. We would pass, exchanging furtive glances. She wouldn't say she knew who I was, and I was afraid to take the first step. The fear of rejection, you know. But her friends told me she watched the show regularly. And so does Irving Berlin. And so did the great General Douglas MacArthur.

Howard Thompson of the *Times* says, "You never know who will turn up—often more effectively than the earlier network talkfests, with their razzle-dazzle." God bless you, Howard, for that. The show is taped, of course, meaning that if Attila the Hun showed up we could scrub it. But the balance of unlikely guests is what makes it click. There was a time, by the way, when I didn't have that sort of answer. At first I was lecturing my viewers, yelling at them, imitating the performers I had seen in this situation. Then one day, God knows why, something happened. The conversational approach took hold. It was like mayonnaise jelling. I felt comfortable. I felt in unison with my guests and in contact with my audience.

There are generally three segments to an hour's show, and we use the breaks to make appropriate adjustments in the order the guests appear and how long they stay on. Some may be on at the start and stay the whole time, with new members of the conversation moving in and out. Others may start and be taken off before the end. Nobody knows, except for those who take precedence because of their own time requirements, or their prestige, when they will be on and when they will go off. At the breaks I survey the guests still waiting in the wings to decide who will work best next. Often I change horses in midstream. Maybe the hypnotist will have something to say to the woman horse trainer, or to that hypnotically sexy blonde actress. I've said it a hundred times: The best conversations in the world aren't scripted—why try to rehearse them just because they're on TV? What is TV best at, anyway?

After I had been on the tube for ten years, I thought I was qualified to answer that question. In the *Sunday*

*News* of July 29, 1962, I volunteered the following prognostications:

> Nostalgia alone will never hold up. When I show an Al Jolson film clip, I immediately balance the books by presenting in person somebody currently high in popularity. Nostalgia alone is a great come-on, but it can become soggy.
>
> I don't have any instruction on the program. Women watching TV don't want to be taught how to cook, sew, or use cosmetics. For this they go to a newspaper or a magazine so that they will have time to pause, reflect, and absorb.

So much for Julia Child, the Galloping Gourmet, Arlene Dahl, "Upstairs, Downstairs," "That's Entertainment," and Barbara Walters. "Pause, reflect, and absorb" sounded so good. But now I see newspapers becoming media for entertainment, and television presenting food for thought.

But what *is* TV best at, anyway?

To look at the salaries, you might say . . . weather reports. Anchormen are, pardon the expression, heavy. It's difficult to compete with sports or soap operas. Ask me. I switched from daytime TV back to the late night and early morning slot just to avoid that kind of competition. And if you think I'm cowardly, ask anyone else in my kind of programming who has tried it both ways.

Television is a difficult medium to come to terms with. People react intensely to it. It corrupts the youth; it's the answer to the problems of reaching the youth. It's chewing gum for the eyes (who said that?); it's McDonald's for the eyes (I said that). Actually, it's more like Nathan's. But who ever expected Nathan's to save the world from hunger?

My hope is that television won't go the way of movies that is, from the highly individual concern of caring people to the child of corporate bookkeepers. Ernie Kovacs was one guy who died with a hope written all over him. I see a resurgence of interest in that kind of character. I dream of the day when bright young people can barge onto a set and create what they know people want. I can see Kovacs giving a weather report, in the manner of a Hungarian: "Hot, svett." Or portraying the blindfold chess champion who not only loses all his games but also knocks over the board in his staggering performance. One doesn't have to bowl everybody over to make a mark in television. But I hope the terrible grip the ratings have on the medium can be eased. I will never understand how 1,500 homes can tell us what 60 million people are watching.

It would be wonderful if radio were to come to the rescue of its younger sister. Now, don't get me wrong. As a performer, I like TV. I like its immediate effect on the audience. It's the closest thing to vaudeville since vaudeville died. At the same time (as the politicians are wont to say), I like the flexibility of radio. By being faceless, it's more receptive to talent that may not have the face. It's also ubiquitous; the portable transistor TV and the car TV are still rare (and the driver can't watch TV anyway). And radio is still a ten-cent paper, not the dollar slick. And something very important—on the creative end of it, people can afford to experiment on radio.

Who said this?—

What could we do without a radio? At any hour of the day or night, tune in and somebody is telling you how to live, how to vote, how to drink, how to think, when to wash your teeth, when to wash your hair, when to cut your whiskers, when to see your doctor, and how to see your doctor, and when to see your priest, and when to see your preacher, and how to put on fat, and how to take it off, and how to make the skin stay white and how to make it stay black.

Honest, no other nation in the world would stand for such advice as that. But we do, and we like it. So the only thing that can make us give up our radio is poverty. The old radio is the last thing to go out of the house when the sheriff comes in.

It's an invention that has knocked nobody out of work and that gives work to many people. That's something you can't say for many inventions. So, as bad as it is, I don't know, it's the best invention I think that has ever been.

If you said Will Rogers, you get an *A* for anthropology. I would like to add that Will was quite a prophet. Neither hi-fi nor TV nor sex in the supermarket have been able to dilute our enthusiasm for radio, spelled in four-letter words, sometimes three.

The things that have meant something for me in life —radio, TV, old films, old records, books, show business—have done it for me because of the human element they contained. Nostalgia is not about old things; it's about the people in old things who remind us that we're not so different. In this chapter I've allowed myself to say everything I want to about myself. To boast.

To take accolades. So now I'd like to show how others are not so different from me.

Rudolph Valentino discussed the subject of pride versus humility in a strange old book he wrote at the peak of his career. "There are hundreds of Valentinos in Italy far more handsome than I can ever hope to be," he wrote from a sojourn in Italy. "Here, I was absolutely in the background." That's a fine sentiment. But I would have preferred something more exuberant, a celebration of what he felt as the idol of American women.

In contrast, I offer Tom Mix's horse. Sometime in the late thirties, I picked up a book called *Tony and His Pals* in a downtown book stall (books about horses should always be picked up in stalls). It had a preface by, get this, a philosophy professor from UCLA. Dr. Starbruck said that children and horses were Tom's very existence, but no rebuttal was allowed from Kierkegaarde. In any event, in one exquisite chapter of that book Tom Mix's horse is allowed to speak in the first person —about pride and humility.

> I have heard that Tom once told a newspaperman that I liked to show off. Well, I'll tell you something. He likes to show off too. Do you think he would do all those difficult and dangerous tricks if he thought nobody would see them? Not likely. And I'm just the same in that respect. I can do clever things and I like it to be known. For that is a quite proper kind of pride.

It's the kind of pride that means self-confidence, when you know someone believes in you. This is what convinces me you should always say yes. "Yes, I *can!*" The horse continues—

> If you ever see me going down a steep or difficult place by myself in a picture, just watch the way my master acts. You will perhaps see me hesitate for a moment, and then you will see him give me a kind of push, and then I will go down. That push means: "Go on down—you know you can do it if you like. What are you waiting for?" And because he believes I can do it, and because he knows that I understand he believes in me, I can always do the things I am set to do.

Another of my cast-off books, *Grey Dawn Reflections* by Virginia Beale Leckie, gave me a more acid view of the pride–humility trade-off. I remember clearly how my eyes fell on a page of acerbic thoughts, decorously staged like poems on heavy vellum stock, before I flipped to the inside cover to determine the price. A nickel. And it bore a 1905 imprint! First there were aphorisms:

> A good looking woman has a right to be vain, and a homely one has to be.

And then some heavier stuff, on flattery—

> Friendship without frankness. It doesn't exist. There is no limit to a man's adoration if you vary and increase in subtlety the modes of flattery. Men marry simple, innocent little women, with baby stares, and then are surprised that the limited sphere of the home aide proves unequal to their expanding ideas.

"The home aide." Why has that phrase lain idle all these years? Yet there is in Ms. Leckie a timeless feeling for juxtaposition of thoughts. That paragraph contains the plot of a novel; it was the dream it inspired in me that made me spend that nickel.

Giorlando Castronovo is a name to reckon with. He is not a film producer, but he's got the talent for that and more. For convenience his father contracted his own name to John Castron; the son retained the original. I know the senior Castronovo because he takes up a chair next to me about six days a week, answers the phone, or, better yet, ends those desperate phone conversations with a brusqueness I'm supposed to have but often can't muster. Now John has already lived his dream. He has spent a half his nearly eighty years as a trainer for fighters, middleweights mostly. He has a zany sense of humor and an enthusiasm for the young and the old. I want to be associated with such people, people who are bursting with courage to face the future. I want to have such people around me, in person or in memory. Their exuberance for life is stirred by their love for people. I'm afraid I flounder in trying to capture the essence of that love, but here allow me at least to dream.